ELDORADO TO THE KLONDIKE

Riding inappropriate motorbikes to out-of-the-way places

NICK ADAMS

CONTENTS

INTRODUCTION

Old or unsuitable motorbikes, distant places, poor weather and gravel roads, these seem to be the common threads in my motorcycle travels. As I was looking through some of my motorcycle trip photographs the other day, it struck me that many of my favourite pictures – indeed a disproportionate number of all the photographs on my computer - were of gravel roads. Now you might reasonably assume that I'm a dirt-bike rider, skilled in blasting through waterholes, over rocky creek beds and along forest tracks, but nothing could be further from the truth. I have no skill or training in riding off-road, the bikes I usually prefer for my trips down the dusty roads are 'standard' touring bikes from the nineteen seventies, and my backside tends to stay resolutely attached to the seat.

Many years ago, long before my passion for motorcycles and riding was revived, I was astonished to meet some riders in northern Ontario who thought nothing of hammering down the hard-packed gravel roads north of Lake Huron on their Harley Shovelheads. Having grown up in England, where even the tiniest lanes are paved, I had assumed that unless you had special skill and special equipment, like the scrambler racers I saw on weekend TV, unpaved gravel roads were no place for a motorbike. I expected the riders to fall off at every corner.

I had driven those roads many times in a truck and was well aware of how the loose surface could have you skittering sideways in a moment unless you were careful. I couldn't imagine how anyone could possibly remain upright on two wheels, yet week after week those riders passed by our house on their way to Friday night drinking sessions at the bar in Bruce Mines. Some hours later, we'd hear them heading back the other way. We called them the 'Drunk Riders'.

Since then I've been drawn to the far corners of the map, the places you can only reach by air unless you drive or ride for many bumpy miles on unpaved surfaces. At first I tended to avoid unpaved roads, but as my confidence grew, I started to ventured further off the tarmac. Once I got used to the feel of not being entirely in control, I began to relax and enjoy the sensation. I quickly found that maintaining a death grip on the handlebars is counterproductive; it is essential to stay loose and let the front wheel find its own path, even when that involves a little skittering and sliding. My experience is that if you keep your speed under control, keep your centre of gravity low by weighting the foot pegs, and use the bike's torque to pull you through any difficulties, you can ride hundreds of miles on gravel in reasonable safety.

Of course, there will be times when things get out of control and a little scary. Patches of deep, loose gravel built up in corners or along the edges of the road are traps which you sometimes can't avoid. You have to grit your teeth and hope that the bike stays upright. Perhaps worse are the deep divots where truck wheels have sunk in to soft, wet gravel and the hole has become filled with loose dust. If you hit one of those there's not much you can do except let the bike bounce around and keep rolling.

Freshly-graded roads look enchanting. Where the road is level, the grader blade tickles the surface, raking it as smooth and appealing as a Zen garden. Unfortunately, all may not be as serene beneath the surface. That perfect-looking road-bed may conceal deep wet spots, dust-filled divots or sharp rocks hidden beneath the powder.

In order to find and explore these roads, sometimes you have to put in a few paved-road miles first. Often many, many miles.............

This book is divided into three quite distinct sections. **Part 1** describes my recent trip to the Arctic Circle and beyond on my 1972 Moto Guzzi Eldorado. This was a trip I had initially hoped to complete in 2017 until a little heart trouble put the brakes on that. Then, just as my body was fully fit, the Eldorado decided to play up. The first few pages describe the sorry story of my own mechanical incompetence until, saved by someone with real skill and patience, the bike emerged ready for the road again.

What I'd initially intended as a few days on the road 'proving' the reliability of the bike suddenly turned into a 22 day, 9000 mile epic. The bike got me home, but not without a few hiccups along the way.

Part 2 is a story of a different nature as for once I'm riding a modern, reliable, efficient two-wheeler. For a long time now the Trans-Labrador Highway has been a 'bucket list' route of choice for many motorcyclist adventurers. There is only one road across Labrador and even now large sections of it are still unpaved. It's a road for big BMW GS's, V-Stroms, Super Tenere's and…………….a scooter?

After two weeks touring in Newfoundland with my wife, I had a choice when she flew home. I could either take the quick way home through Nova Scotia, New Brunswick and Quebec, or the long-way-round through Labrador. Guess which I chose?

Part 3 starts with a monologue about the joys of the first ride of the year, then is followed by an account of an early spring ride on my Guzzi Convert automatic. The Convert was an odd duck in the nineteen seventies and it hasn't become any less unusual since. Many riders discount automatic motorcycles as somehow not providing the full opportunity to exercise skill and control. They have no idea what they're missing.

I don't set out with the intention of riding unusual bikes to distant places, but it turns out that that is what I seem to do. I like the bikes I ride and I like the places I go. Put the two together and, well, you end up with stories like these.

………………………………..

PART 1
ELDORADO TO THE KLONDIKE

SHE'S A FICKLE LADY

I've had a love affair with my 1972 Moto Guzzi Eldorado ever since I bought her twelve years ago. I've only recently started to refer to it as 'her'. It used to be that I didn't have any sense that a mechanical object could have a gender but, as the years and miles have added up, her character has emerged and there is no question in my mind that she is a 'she'. Nowadays I think of her as a once-stunning Italian lady, now, at 47, starting to show her age a little, but still undeniably a head-turner. In the same way that Hollywood often characterizes women of a certain age – especially those from southern European countries – as caring, but also tempestuous, vengeful and strident, so my Eldorado, though mainly admirable, has a vindictive side which started when I first brought another bike into my garage, and has continued unabated. Nevertheless, despite being a little high-maintenance, she has never really let me down and has taken me on many long rides to remote and interesting places, so the following litany of problems and repairs came as a surprise.

After a long winter, I pulled her out of the garage for a quick ride. There was still plenty of snow around, but the roads were clear of snow and ice, and even though the temperatures were well below what most people would consider reasonable for riding, I just couldn't wait. It wasn't a long ride – just enough to get the oil circulating and for me to remember how much I enjoyed it after a months of being housebound. I left her running while I took a couple of pictures, and after removing my earplugs

I could hear a disturbing sound that hadn't been there (or I hadn't noticed) the previous autumn.

Assuming it was the clutch rod bearing, I ordered a new one. In the meantime I partially disassembled the rear of the bike so I had the space to extract the old one and replace it with the new. Time passed, the parts arrived and were installed. No change. The noise was still there.

HAPPIER DAYS

Next I thought it must be the clutch, even though the action of the clutch was perfect. Perhaps a bolt had worked loose or a spring had cracked. You can tell I was fishing for easy answers.

Because the Guzzi has an automotive-style dry clutch, it's necessary to remove the gearbox, and to do that the rear wheel, swinging arm and a host of other bits. No problem, I'd done it before and it's all simple, logical stuff. With the gearbox out I took the clutch to pieces and inspected it carefully. The bolts had all been tight and there were no broken springs. It must be a problem in the gearbox.

At this point I should mention that, since buying the Eldorado, I'd personally ridden her for almost 65,000 miles and her total mileage was just a few miles shy of 100,000. I was eager to get over that big hump and start towards 200,000. Throughout that time the gearbox had been flawless, although I had been noticing lately that it was getting a little reluctant to shift into some of the gears and slipped out of first from time to time.

I thought rebuilding a gearbox was beyond my mechanical ability, but some of the Guzzi fanatics on an internet forum convinced me that it was a very simple box and that with sufficient care, anyone should be able to do it. Not so! I took the gearbox to pieces, had some of the bearings replaced by my local machine shop, and reassembled it. I put it back in the bike, rode down the road, and promptly came to a grinding, sliding halt as it locked up solidly. Who knows what I had done wrong. Obviously something critical.

Over the next few weeks I searched around and eventually found a person suitably experienced with Moto Guzzi innards to rebuild my gearbox. Yves's business lay 170 miles away but he had decades of experience with Moto Guzzis and came highly recommended by a fellow whose opinion I trust (except on politics, but that's a different matter).

Yves carefully went through my gearbox finding stripped gears and other damage, finally declaring that I would be better off getting a replacement. Through the marvels of eBay he was able to source one in the US, check it over and service it. Not long afterwards I had it bolted back on the bike and was heading down the road. At first all seemed strange as the 'new' gearbox was from a later model and had the one down four up pattern that has become common to all bikes now. My old Eldorado had a one up four down pattern, so until I figured it out I was a bit confused. That was the least of my worries though.

Whether from being locked up solid when the gearbox failed, Italian spite, or coincidence, the now perfect gearbox was being turned by an engine which had developed a nasty knock. I couldn't determine the source of the knock, but it was deep, obvious, and wouldn't go away. Out came the bike lift and the wrenches again. Out came the gearbox, then out came the engine. Once again, I was heading down the highway to Yves's place. This time with the back of my station wagon full of engine parts.

To cut a long and involved story a bit shorter, Yves discovered that the problem lay in the left-side piston which had been clattering against the barrel wall. I opted to go for new pistons and nikisil barrels. He recommended a new oil pump, so one of those was ordered and installed too. Incredibly, despite almost 100,000 miles the whole bottom end of the engine was in 'like new' condition, showing no signs of wear.

Eventually the day came when I was able to retrieve my engine and start reassembling the bike. All went absurdly smoothly, if you overlook the small but critical clutch part that I'd omitted, forcing me to take it all apart once more. Finally, though, the bike was running, the gears were working, new oil was in all the right places. It was time for that first ride. It was glorious. I only went a few miles. The bike felt and sounded fantastic. Spending all that money had been worth it. The bike felt reborn. I headed home.

Half-way up the Loughborough Lake hill I felt a judder and heard a grinding noise coming from the rear. I eased off the throttle and carried on. Then it happened again. There was something amiss in the rear drive box. Had I forgotten the gear oil. I prayed I hadn't.

After limping home I extracted the rear drive box and looked inside. There was gear oil all right, only now it glittered with aluminum bits and the drain plug magnet was coated in steel. Despite their tab washers, two of the bolts which hold the bevel gears in place had backed out until their heads had started to collide with the aluminium webbing on the case. It was a mess. The bolts had sheared and the webbing was in tatters.

I cleaned the mess up as best I could and examined the bevel gears. Incredibly, they were unmarked. Not a scratch, not a chipped tooth to be seen. I drilled out the broken bolts, re-tapped the holes and reassembled the drive box, using good tab washers and copious amounts of thread-locker. With the wheel back on and new gear oil and molybdenum additive in the drive, I gave it a spin. Smooth as silk. No nasty grinding or crunching noises at all.

With everything stitched back together, I started the Eldorado and took it for a quick spin around the block. Everything seemed to be working well.

I dropped my friend Phil an email:

"Do you want to meet for lunch tomorrow? Haliburton? About 12ish?"

"Sure. Riding the Eldo?"

"Yep".

Haliburton is about equidistant between where Phil lives in Ancaster and where I live. It would be roughly 175 miles each way for both of us, although I got the better part of the deal. Phil had to navigate around the urban chaos of Toronto, while I had country roads the whole way.

If you're keyed up for yet another tale of roadside disaster, I'm sorry to disappoint you. The Eldorado behaved flawlessly and was running so well that Phil and I even explored a few back roads together before parting company again for the journey home.

The newly rebuilt engine is very slightly smoother than its former self. Things were looking good. I guessed it would take a little while for the new pistons to bed in and fully loosen up, and there would be plenty of time for the old girl to act up as the miles piled on. I was delighted to have my Eldorado back in road-worthy trim and ready for some new adventures.

Now, where's my road atlas.

WHERE ARE YOU HEADING?

I left home near Kingston, Ontario before 5AM on the last Friday in June, generally heading west. To paraphrase Gord Downie in that terrific bike road movie, **'One Week'**, *'I had Direction but not Destination'*. The first day was uneventful, except the darn bike was reluctant to idle on both cylinders and would buck and splutter at low speed. Never mind, though, there's not much call for idling between home and my mate Ken's home in Webbwood, near the north shore of Lake Huron.

On the first day, after a few hours of pleasant riding, I stopped for a coffee at the Tim Hortons in Mattawa. As I checked my phone messages, through the window I could see a couple of guys inspecting my bike. I'd seen them arrive just before me – two couples on big modern twins, loaded for a big tour. The ladies were taking advantage of the cool air inside, but the Eldorado was working its usual magic as a guy magnet. I'd finished fiddling with my phone, so I grabbed my coffee and went outside to join them where we chatted about our respective trips. They were heading to Edmonton and the Icefields Parkway – a magnificent road which runs for 144 miles through the Rocky Mountains between Jasper and Banff. I was still unsure of my heading. I may have said something about gravel roads north of Highway 11, as I had no real plans and was still getting used to the refreshed engine.

People often look at my bike, quietly thinking to themselves that they wouldn't trust it around the block. The paint is worn and missing in a few places, my gear is held on with a plethora of bungees, and, with nice loose tappets, it sounds like two bags of nails being shaken in a bucket. It would be unfair of me to assume that that was what these guys were thinking, but I wouldn't be surprised.

As I left Tim's heading towards North Bay, I began to think about mountains. I hadn't seen much of the Rockies and had only seen a small part of British Columbia's Coastal Range when I'd taken my youngest son of a very short trip to BC a few years before. Mountains......hmmm.

At Ken's that first evening we spent a pleasant hour being bug bitten while we tried to sort the carbs, set the ignition timing accurately and gap the points. We'd thought we had it nailed, but as I headed back toward the Trans-Canada highway in the morning the Eldorado was spluttering and would only run well if I kept the revs up.

'Oh well, she'll sort herself out when she gets warmed up', I thought. Wrong. I had hardly gone 5 miles when the misfiring got much worse and then she died altogether. I pulled onto the soft shoulder.

After years of riding old bikes, I'm smart enough to keep a comprehensive tool kit near the top of the pannier. Still thinking it was carb problems I was just about to pull the top off the right-hand Del Orto when I noticed that the capacitor, which is usually bolted to the side of the distributor (what? your bike doesn't have a distributor?), was hanging by a couple of threads of one of the bolts. The other bolt had vanished. I tightened it up, the bike started and sounded good. So we set off again – for the next 20 miles – until the bike staggered to a stop again. This time the remaining bolt had vibrated free.

In my bag of spare bits, I had multiple old sets of points (what? your bike doesn't have points?), one of which had the little bolt which, as luck, or great Guzzi forethought would have it, was the size I needed. It was a bit of a fiddle to get the bolt into the little holes. Various carb parts and HT leads are in the way, so of course I dropped the precious bolt.

Back to my tool kit for the magnet-on-a-stick. You can tell I've been there before. I went fishing for the dropped bolt and came up with two. One of the originals had lodged in a little depression in the crankcase. Eventually I got one bolted in place. I dropped the other in the gravel and despite fishing with the magnet for a while I couldn't find it.

Oh well, these things happen. To prevent the remaining bolt from going walk-about again, I slapped some Gorilla tape over the condenser, pressing it firmly down over the nut.

I passed through Sault Ste. Marie before mid-day and was soon heading north up the spectacular Lake Superior coast. I've ridden the Trans-Canada Highway between Sault Ste. Marie and Thunder Bay numerous times. It's an enjoyable ride and can be very scenic as long as the mists off the lake aren't shrouding all the hills and filling all the valleys. Where the highway rises over headlands it's often far warmer than back down at lake level where cool air off Lake Superior is hanging about. I had pulled the quilted liner out of my leather jacket and stuffed it under the bungees, so alternately I wished I was wearing it, and was glad I wasn't.

HEADING WEST BUT STILL IN ONTARIO

The road rises over immense rocky headlands, past lakes, innumerable rock cuts and countless billions of trees, before diving back down to lake level again and again. I stopped a few times to take some pictures, and briefly stopped to say hello and give a hug to my youngest son who's a Park Warden at Pancake Bay Provincial Park. Most of the time though, I was just riding along listening to the sound of the engine and the wind noise as the miles accumulated. Eventually my stamina started to flag. I pulled into a motel in Terrace Bay, had a quick supper in the bar and turned in.

I still wasn't sure where I was heading, but by this time I couldn't even pretend I wasn't headed west. I suppose I wasn't prepared to admit to myself that what I'd described to my wife as 'probably a four or five day trip', was gradually morphing into something more.

On long rides, if there's any traffic at all, it's easy to fall into highway-zombie mode where you feel driven along because you don't want to be passed by all the vehicles you just overtook. It's too easy to zip along, never stopping, rarely resting, until suddenly the ride is over and you can barely remember it. I rode around Lake Superior and across to the Manitoba border in highway-zombie mode. Just getting through Ontario had become the first step. My confidence that the Eldorado was unlikely to explode beneath me was increasing and I was beginning to think about the west.

ACROSS THE PRAIRIES

Ever since I read some of the early explorer's accounts, the far west and, especially, the lands above the tree line have fascinated me. Perhaps because I grew up in a country where all the hilltops are bare, I tend to feel a little claustrophobic in a world dominated by trees, and ache for endless views, open windswept hills and scenery rolling off to the far horizon. Small steps though. Don't think too far ahead. One province at a time. I passed through the Ontario/Manitoba border at about 5PM that Sunday afternoon. Next stop Saskatchewan.

The 'Welcome to Manitoba' sign is plastered with stickers. It looks like just about every motorcyclist that passes that way stops to take a picture, then plasters some logo sticker on the base of the sign. I stopped to take a picture but wasn't carrying any stickers. It seemed a bit silly – a bit like the saying 'I was here', as if anyone cared.

The folks at the Manitoba Information building were extremely helpful. With their free map I was guided away from the Trans-Canada Highway towards Highway 44 – the old Highway 1. This road scoots past the touristy area near West Hawk Lake, then almost immediately turns into a quiet, roughly-paved, twisty road through the Whiteshell Provincial Forest. This wasn't the boring, endlessly flat Manitoba I'd been told to expect. This was nice. This was fun.

It had been another long day. While I paid for my fuel in the small community of Rennie, I asked the guy behind the cash if there were any motels near by. He pointed to the ratty-looking 'Rennie Hotel' across the street. "It's close, and it's cheap". I had assumed it was just a bar, but according to him, they did have rooms available too.

The two young guys at the desk weren't sure that the one room available had been cleaned yet. I was just about to offer to use my sleeping bag and to heck with changing the bedding, when they decided that it had, and was mine for $50 for the night. There was a bed, an air conditioner that functioned, even a TV. It was a bit sketchy, but for $50 for the night I could do sketchy – and anyway, there was beer in the bar downstairs. Perfect!

RENNIE, MANITOBA

It didn't take long before I'd left the delightful part of the road behind and encountered what I'd been expecting: manicured fields extending off into the distant horizon, broad, straight roads and virtually no traffic. I suppose the latter was to be expected as I was back in the saddle by 6AM on the Canada Day long weekend, when most sensible people were still in bed. The posted road speed limit was 100kph but I found I preferred to hum along at a steady 90-95. This had nothing to do with the Guzzi which is perfectly capable of cruising at much higher speeds, but I found the lower wind noise relaxing, while I was still making good progress. Very occasionally I'd see a vehicle in my rear-view mirror, then almost immediately it would whoosh past. Clearly, obeying posted speed limits was regarded as optional in Manitoba.

I'd been hoping to start the day with a coffee and perhaps a muffin at Beausejour, but I managed to sail past and was in Lockport before I knew it, having crossed over the enormous Red River spillway before touching the town. I was on the look-out for a coffee shop but as I crossed the bridge above St. Andrews dam something caught my eye which had me doing a U-turn in the middle of the bridge. In the rapids below the dam were Pelicans – great rafts of them – floating downstream with the flow, then getting a free ride back in the strong eddies. I parked the bike and headed down to water's edge, watching in delight and amazement as they coordinated their fishing – each bird plunging its head into the water at the same time. It was going to be a bird day. I'd already seen a Bald Eagle in the sky above and a pair of Sandhill Cranes hunting along a railroad track and there were more to come. In my excitement of seeing the Pelicans I forgot all about finding a coffee so continued heading north-west up the Interlakes region between Lake Winnipeg and Lake Manitoba.

Instead of topping up in Teulon, which was a far smaller community than the size of text on my map would suggest, I carried on. Although I'd started with a full tank of fuel, it was becoming obvious that finding anywhere open on a holiday Monday was going to be a bit of an issue. The bike started to stumble as I pulled in to Poplarfield. This didn't mean much. The Eldorado drains one side of the fuel tank first, leaving a substantial reserve on the other side. I usually ride until the bike stutters then switch on the right-side fuel tap and carry on.

On the journey so far, I had filled the tank whenever I was near a gas station and hadn't paid much attention to the cost or volume, so had no real idea of fuel consumption. When I first had the bike, it would reliably return 50+ miles to the Imperial gallon, but its consumption had got steadily worse as the miles accumulated and the engine became worn. I had yet to determine what (if any) difference the new cylinders and pistons would make.

Inevitably, the gas station in Poplarfield was shut. I pulled into the parking area and was reaching for the 10 litre fuel jug on my rear rack when a young guy pulled up in a pick-up. He was polite enough, but gave me one of those ' What are you up to' looks. I wondered whether he was an off-duty cop, or just a nosy – no, curious – local. With my reserve supply poured into the tank I was feeling a bit less insecure, especially when he told me that the gas station/restaurant 'at the highway' was a mere 24 miles to the west. The gas station was open. It was 11.47 AM when I sat down for my first food and drink of the day.

Manitoba turned out to be exactly as described: mostly flat farmland, endlessly straight, beautifully surfaced roads, and incredibly sparsely populated. Occasionally I'd pass a farm or a bungalow set well back from the road, but usually there were just miles and miles of open farm fields and the sporadic scattering of cows. I hadn't given much thought to the bike for ages. It continued to sing a happy song as the miles passed under her wheels. Hours went by without a single gear change or variation in speed. This part of Manitoba – indeed much of northwestern Ontario, Manitoba and Saskatchewan – lie within the lake-bed of the massive post-glacial Lake Agassiz which lay trapped between ice to the north and higher land to the south. Despite their gargantuan sizes, the lakes that now dominate central Manitoba – Lake Winnipeg,

Lake Manitoba and Lake Winnipegosis – are mere puddles compared to what used to be here.

This is a big country. I've said it before and will probably say it again before I lay my head in my own bed once more. The next day's ride dispensed with Manitoba, crossed the entire province of Saskatchewan and ended in Viking, Alberta - a total of 511 grinding miles. That's not a record shattering distance - I've ridden many longer days - but this one was into a strong, constant headwind that ground this rider to a pulp and turned the poor Eldorado into a total gas hog. I had to resort to my spare can a couple of times. While the bike's huge fairing gave me some relief, the poor thing took a terrific buffeting every time a truck went by and was constantly under strain. I realized I was giving Saskatchewan short-shrift but with such a strong wind I was more intent on struggling through than being observant or lyrical.

Even without a persistent headwind, there's no doubt that riding across the prairies is an exercise in endurance. Straight roads go on for so many miles that they would make the Romans proud, although even the Romans would have been aching for an excuse to throw in a bend or two. While the scenery does change, the transitions are decidedly gradual. It's tempting, after a single pass-through, to think, 'Well, that's all I need to see of the prairies', and it's true that I'll be happy not to ride the same route again. But I kept seeing appealing little roads heading off into the distance, especially in western Saskatchewan, which had far more topography than I expected. Its low ridges, swales, sloughs and ponds mixed with massive farm fields and the occasional grain elevator thrown in for good measure, were surprisingly charming.

If you took the English county of Norfolk, removed everything built before 1900, eliminated half the villages, grabbed it by the corners and stretched it until it covered an area the size of the Iberian peninsula, then dropped it down in the middle of North America, you'd have an approximation of the prairies. Distances between communities are huge, and when you get there there's no darn gas pump, or if there is, it's a Cardlock system and you don't have the magic key.

Larger communities are better served. Whether they have fuel for desperate travellers is moot, but you can be almost certain that they will have an immense farm machinery dealership, with countless millions of dollars worth of shiny machines lined up row upon row like an outsized suburban Chevy dealership. I saw one called 'Combine World' (I kid you not). You can just imagine the brash TV ad-men telling you that the savings are 'Huge'!

You have a lot of time to think on these roads as the riding isn't exactly demanding. Oh look, there's a corner coming. You probably spotted it from a couple of kilometers away. Most are vast, sweeping bends where the road takes a ninety degree turn over the course of half a county.

And yet.........I liked it.

Little things pleased me: the elk grazing contentedly in a field just on the outskirts of a small town, the endless ducks, sooty terns, cattle egrets and pelicans I saw going about their business in the many sloughs, the generally excellent condition of the roads, and a total absence of roadside garbage. I know there are few people to make a mess, but it seems, they just don't do it. What capped the day for me was seeing not one, but two separate pronghorn antelope. Most of the prairie may have been converted to farmland, but it seems there is still room for some wildlife.

ALBERTA

My first act after crossing into Alberta was to take a pee. Now before anyone starts accusing me of being a snotty Easterner making a political statement, I wasn't. I had stopped to take the obligatory 'bike by provincial sign' picture and as soon as I stopped, my bladder, which I had subconsciously been suppressing for miles, suddenly manifested its need vociferously. I parked the bike strategically close to the sign then ducked into the little stand of poplar bushes.

Could I detect any differences between eastern Alberta and western Saskatchewan? Not really. Not at first anyway. The road surface was a little rougher for the first few miles, but, after Wainwright, Highway 14 was in the process of being repaved, so no room for complaints there. Anyway, by that point in the day I was so beaten by the wind that I didn't have much energy for sight-seeing or creative observation. I just need a place to stop, a shower and a bed. Viking – named after a couple of Norwegians who settled here in 1909 – serviced those needs at the rambling Caledonian Motor Inn. The inn also acted as the community beer dispensary so I was able to purchase a six-pack of Samuel Adams to give me inspiration while I twiddled and adjusted a few things on the bike. In the end, I could only stomach three before the need to sleep overtook me.

The next morning it only took about an hour and a half before I was deep in Edmonton traffic, working my way south from the Yellowhead Trail towards the heart of the city. Such riding conditions aren't my favourite at the best of times, but with a balky bike .... well, let's just say it wasn't one of the highlights of the trip. Google Maps led me to the address I was looking for and I found my Guzzi Angel.

The previous evening I'd done my best to trouble-shoot my idling problem. I wondered whether the condenser wire was arcing against the distributor body, so for good measure I swapped it for one in my spares bag, adjusted the points again and spent a fruitless half-hour playing around with the carbs, trying to find that sweet place where both cylinders chime in. Eventually I gave up. The bike runs. Good enough.

There are some people in this world who are wonderful. I met another one on this day. I'll call him Jim, because that's his name. Bikes seem to bring out the best in people anyway, but I suspect Jim is special all the time. Without giving too much away or causing him embarrassment, let's just say I spent a happy morning watching a true old-bike expert go through my bike, throwing good parts at it, which he stole from one of the bikes in his own magnificent collection. By the time we finished, my Eldorado was sporting a completely new cap-and-plug lead set, a new condenser and two shiny, fully functioning carbs. Needless to say, it idles smoothly and runs like a train. Of course, all this didn't come without strings. While we worked on the bike, Jim told me about some of his many road trips and got me all fired up about heading further north and west. In the end I made a promise (or at least a commitment) to ride the old Eldorado to Dawson City. So that became the plan.

Before I go any further, let's just let that sink in for a while. It had taken me just over five days to ride from home to Edmonton – a distance of roughly 2200 miles. Now, I was signing up to ride to Dawson City. It's all very well thinking, 'Well, Edmonton is in western Canada, so how much further can it be?' The answer is, 'Quite a lot'. By the most direct route, it's almost 1600 miles to Dawson City. It was starting to look as though I would be venturing a long way from home on my old bike. Still, adhering to the pop-psyche mantra of 'Wherever you go, there you are', I figured that one patch of deserted road was pretty much the same as another, so where I broke down wouldn't make much difference. That makes it sound as though I was a bit worried. I wasn't really. I had tools and spares, experience and plenty of knowledge of the bike's foibles. We'd be OK.

Since my rear tire was starting to show a little wear, before I left Edmonton I diverted to Alberta Cycle where I bought the only 4 by 18inch tire they had in stock. When the guy behind the counter brought it out my heart sank. I had been hoping for an ordinary street tire – something that would last up to Dawson City and also get me home. Instead, I was presented with an aggressive knobbly – the kind you might put on the rear of your 250cc dirt bike to go ripping up the trails. Oh well, better than nothing I suppose, and at $60 the price was right, although I assumed it would wear out fast. I bungeed the knobbly on to the back of the bike and headed out of the city.

HEADING TO THE MOUNTAINS

A couple of things came to mind as I rolled up the 'scenic route' from Hinton to Grande Prairie, then along the far less scenic, and definitely less interesting lower section of the Alaska Highway between Dawson Creek and Fort St. John, then along the slightly more scenic, but still rather dull few hundred miles north of Fort St. John. The first thing was the rather surprising lack of roadkill. I saw one large buck being turned into crow food at the side of the road, and a porcupine or two, but little else. Except, that is, for one rather sad sight. A small bear cub had failed to quite make it across the highway. He was face down, legs splayed and a bit flattened, but not yet pulverized to a grease stain. His jet-black fur and pretty feet were in startling contrast to the red inside parts – he looked more like a child's stuffed toy than something that, until a few hours before, had been living and breathing.

But I'm being uncharitable, dismissive and ignorant about a whole vast territory just because it didn't inflame my passion for dramatic landscape. As I approached where the Alaska Highway crosses the Peace River I can remember thinking that although I'd heard about the Peace River district ever since I'd been in Canada, I really had no idea where it was or what it was like. I could see that farming was a big deal, but I now know that the lands surrounding the Peace River contain some of the most northerly productive and fertile farm-lands in the country. The Peace River itself is a mighty watercourse which is over 1000 miles long and one of the major tributaries of the MacKenzie, while the MacKenzie, one of those rivers that few outside Canada have ever heard of, has a drainage basin second only in size to the Mississippi in North America, and is the thirteenth longest in the world.

PEACE RIVER VALLEY

The Peace River valley is a huge gash across an otherwise fairly level landscape and the road winds down the valley edge in a series of broad, steep curves. I stopped at a pull-in to see if I could get a satisfactory picture but wasn't happy with the results and quickly moved on, crossing the river on the Taylor Bridge, a contentious metal structure subject to constant maintenance and repairs. This constant attention is a good thing. The original suspension bridge collapsed in 1957.

The second observation concerns the other bikes on the road, of which I had seen relatively few — just two or three small groups of riders, on everything from sport tourers to KLRs. I would have thought, with so few bikes passing in either direction, that one would be happy to extend a wave to fellow travellers, yet about fifty percent of the riders I passed didn't even flicker a finger or share a nod. I pondered on this. Perhaps, if heading up the Alaska Highway is your big adventure (it certainly was a big adventure for me), maybe you want to maintain the illusion that what you've done (or are doing) is somehow unique and special and the last thing you want to see is some old git riding an old clunker. On the other hand, perhaps half the folks riding the Alaska Highway are prats. I'll let you know if I ever figure it out.

The people who impressed me most were the solitary cyclists I saw from time to time, their bicycles burdened with panniers front and rear, grinding up those long hills, all sinew and muscle from weeks on the road. No credit card relaxation at motels and restaurants for those folks. The distances between places with even the most limited services meant that they must be camping most of the time. My hat, or at least my helmet, is off to them.

THE ALASKA HIGHWAY

I think I finally hit my stride along the Alaska Highway. Despite twelve hours in the saddle (minus a couple of brief coffee/food/gas stops) my backside didn't ache, my shoulder and neck didn't feel as though they were being skewered with hot knives, and my knees and hands decided not to lock up. No matter how long I rode, a few miles short of 500 seems to be about what I could comfortably squeeze into a day. I would start out with ambition to put in some big mileage days, but by late afternoon I would find myself looking at the map, trying to establish whether to stay put, or throw in another few miles on the off chance that there would be food and fuel at the next inhabited place.

That night, for instance, I was ready to stop at Wonowon. I inquired about a room at a massive construction camp and would have happily bunked down in one of the industrial trailer units, but as I only had plastic and they could only take cash, it wasn't to be. Instead, I rode the extra 40 miles to Pink Mountain and the Buffalo Motor Inn. It's no five-star palace – although the room price might make you think it should be - but it was warm, dry, had hot water, an all-you-can-eat buffet, a bison head in the lounge and a rack to leave your muddy work boots on in the hallway. What more could a fella ask for?

The portion of the Alaska highway between Fort Nelson and Watson Lake is probably the part most people who drive or ride it remember, long after they are comfortably seated back in their own living room. It was certainly true for me, as it was spectacular for two reasons. It's along this stretch of road that you first come face-to-face with real mountains. As you ride west through forested hills along the Tetsa River for a few miles.

Then, quite suddenly, you are in the middle of the aptly named Stone Mountains: bare rounded lumps with barely any signs of vegetation on their upper slopes – the very edge of the northern Rockies. This is stunning scenery and quite unlike anything that I'd seen in the preceding days. I began to feel as though I really was getting towards the north-west. A little further on, the road skirts the beautiful Muncho Lake with the water on one side and steep rock precipices on the other, many of which were draped in netting to help save travellers from falling rocks.

It was also along this stretch that I first encountered the astonishing abundance of wildlife that I had been told about but hadn't fully believed. Within Stone Mountain Park, at close range, I saw a pair of caribou (as my wife insists – in their high-heeled shoes), and a group of mountain sheep. Away from the rocky sections, the road is separated from the surrounding forest by a broad swath of grass which I presume is maintained to give road-users a sporting chance of seeing the wildlife before hitting it. It needs it. Black bears were scattered around like confetti. I stopped to video a large black bear eating grass and soon after, another. A little further on a vehicle ahead of me slowed and a colossal black bear – the biggest I've ever seen, and I've seen many - sauntered across the road. He was in no hurry at all. He was absolutely sure that he was the meanest s-o-b in the forest. I slowed to take a good look at him and catch a frame or two with one of my Gopro cameras. He walked parallel to the highway. He was long and gleaming black, with an almost serpentine neck and head. Paint him white and he would have passed for a polar bear. Magnificent!

A couple of times cinnamon black bear cubs skipped across the road ahead of me. Both times I slowed, waiting for the mother to appear, but either she had already passed or was hanging back just within the tree-line. I also encountered a very pungent dead one. I saw it at the side of the road, slowed, and circled back for a closer look but soon regretted it. He was swelling in the sun and extremely malodorous.

Further on, I passed a simple road sign showing a single bison. It didn't need further explanation as, soon enough, I came across a group of five adults lying in hollows at the side of the road, one of which proceeded to wallow in the dust as I shut off the bike. It's an odd thing but, as soon as the bike was quiet, the wallowing bison fixed his eye firmly fixed on me – a decidedly unnerving experience. I quickly turned the key, started the bike, moved off and thereafter remembered to leave it idling whenever I was watching wildlife.

Soon after, I encountered a much larger group of bison, peacefully grazing or lying about, looking like a herd of Holsteins. But these are not domestic cattle. They are completely wild, melting into the surrounding forest with astonishing ease. It's hard to convey just how immense these animals are. Hitting them with anything smaller than a transport truck would have dire consequences for the driver and passengers. When two large bulls decided to swagger across the road like a pair of self-confident body-builders, the vehicles ahead of me slowed to a crawl and gave them whatever space they needed. They are truly awesome, breath-taking beasts.

The Eldorado continued to soldier on, happily droning for hours at normal road speed, but grumpy and difficult to manage at idle. The Veglia instruments used on many Moto Guzzis have a well-deserved reputation for being a little enthusiastic, but I had to chuckle as I looked down at mine. The speedo was telling me that we were devouring the road at somewhere between 100 and 120 miles per hour, whereas I could tell from the engine noise and the little speedometer app on my phone that we were travelling at a much more moderate 90kph. The tach is equally unreliable. One moment it seems to be telling the truth before veering wildly around into the red zone. I no longer bothered with it. I had stuck the holder for my phone on its glass face.

Before long I reached Watson Lake in the Yukon Territory. I filled the bike with fuel, bought some food and beer at the grocery store from a very nice German lady, and lingered for a few moments outside the sign-post forest before deciding that it really wasn't my kind of thing. I headed for the territorial campsite a few miles down the road. I'd been intending to switch tires that evening. My rear was getting a bit worn. Perhaps I should rephrase that. My rear tire was getting a bit worn, but as I pitched my tent and started to relax, all enthusiasm for tearing the bike apart vapourized. There'd be time enough later on. Instead, I used my phone to order a couple of new tires from Fortnine to be mailed to Jim's address in Edmonton, to be picked up on my return for the journey home.

I almost always sleep well in a tent and this night was no exception. I even awoke a little later than I would have liked, so it was well past 7AM by the time I'd packed my gear, packed the bike and started off down the gravel road back to the highway. As I had a full tank of gas there was no need to back-track to Watson Lake. I headed west again, crossing the substantial Upper Liard River soon after leaving town.

I noticed that even in quite isolated areas people had written their names or constructed other messages in cobbles along the sides of the road. They were everywhere – often quite elegantly done. Who were these people who had taken the time to leave their vehicles and play with arranging rocks? The same folks who build those little Inukshuks everywhere or spray paint their names on any exposed rock surface I suppose. It's a big scary world – perhaps if you put your stamp upon it, it feels less scary. I find Inukshuks and graffiti vaguely pathetic, but, for no apparent reason I found the cobble names oddly endearing and stopped to take a few pictures of the best examples. Don't expect logic – it's just how I feel.

As I was fumbling with my camera, a couple rolled up on a touring Harley. They looked quite concerned and asked whether everything was all right. It's true that shortly before I had been twiddling with the left side carb air screw, and I expect they saw me leaning over the bike. I thanked them for stopping but explained I was just taking some pictures and the bike was fine. One of the slight irritations of riding an older bike in out-of-the-way places is that people assume that, if you're stopped by the side of the road, something must be wrong. It rarely is, and even if it is, it's usually something that can be fixed with a bit of tape, a bungee, the turn of a screw or the application of a little emery paper. Modern bikes don't tend to break down, but how many of their riders have the first clue about what to do if they did? How do you fix a fried ECU or a blown fuel pump at the side of the road when you're not carrying any tools, you're out of cell phone range, and wouldn't know where to start looking for a problem anyway? One can put too much trust in modern technology.

The kind Harley riders rode on and, as I was done with playing camera man, I started the bike again and was soon rolling. I could see the Harley in the distance, so I sped up until I was about 200 metres back and visible in their mirrors to dispel any lingering concerns they might have that I was still stuck at the side of the road. Later that day I bumped into them again at a gas pump. Nice couple. On their way to Alaska from Minnesota. I would see them again.

It finally occurred to me that, if I wanted to do any servicing or tweaking of the bike, I would have to find places away from other's eyes. Otherwise I'd have a constant stream of generous-minded people stopping to offer assistance. When I'd left Edmonton a few days before, the Eldorado had been running well, but as the miles piled on that annoying problem reappeared. At normal road speed the bike was a champ, but if I slowed it would splutter and backfire again. I tucked the bike out of view behind some trees and started to play. The old adage that most carb problems are ignition problems seemed true (little did I know how true this was – but more of this much later). After pointlessly twiddling the air and mixture screws to no effect I finally checked under the distributor cap. The points had almost closed up. How it was running at all was a mystery, yet it had been happily romping along for hour after hour. I gapped the points by eye and started her again. Steady idle speed and reasonable power – not a bad results. A few miles later I stopped again and closed the points to something closer to factory recommendations. That did the trick. Good idle - full power. You've got to love a bike that will trudge on for hours with its most basic settings completely out of whack.

THE KLONDIKE HIGHWAY

Eventually I made it to Whitehorse and lingered at the side of the road in the downtown core, checking my phone for the nearest Tim's. I saw little to entice me to stay downtown and was soon gulping down a bowl of chili served by an attractive young lady whom I guessed might be a Filipino temporary foreign worker. It had been a long time since I'd eaten anything and the chili, bun and coffee were cheap and satisfying. Feeling far less empty, I got back on the bike, got briefly lost in Whitehorse's box-store-world, then found the Alaska Highway again.

Just outside Whitehorse the Alaska Highway veers to the west and the Klondike Highway splits north. I'd barely crossed the Takhini River bridge when I noticed the headlight of a motorbike closing fast in my mirror. Since I was happy to travel at a leisurely pace, I assumed that the rider would soon blast past. But no, he tucked in behind me and sat on my tail — far enough behind to be polite, but close enough to leave no doubt that we had become an item. My curiosity was tweaked. I tried to recognize the type of bike, but with only the headlight to go by, it didn't prove possible. I endured this for about twenty miles until my curiosity could stand it no longer. I pulled over on the pretext that I was going to take a photograph of the interesting green water in the adjacent lake. My shadow slowed too, then pulled alongside flipping up his visor and introducing himself. This was Jerry, from Florida. He was riding a V-Strom loaded like a goldfield pack-mule and had been on the road for ages. Not surprisingly, he too was a little curious about my bike, since it was obvious that it was loaded for some serious traveling, heading north on the Klondike Highway, and obviously not just out for the day. After chatting for a while, Jerry sped off and I doggedly continued to roll north at my own comfortable speed. I had a feeling we would meet again.

MY SHADOW: JERRY

I'd first noticed the Yukon River in Whitehorse. Well, it was rather hard to miss if, like me, you'd temporarily abandoned the Alaska Highway and headed downtown on the Robert Service Way, as the road runs right next to the river at the base of its shaly clay banks. I'd seen it again as I first set off up the Klondike Highway, but, either I wasn't paying attention or I had other things on my mind, because it really didn't fizz on me until I saw it at Carmacks.

Even at Carmacks, I stopped for fuel and crossed the big steel bridge, hardly noticing the enormous river. Almost immediately, I pulled in to the 'Coal Mine Campground and Canteen' to buy an ice cream, which had been in my thoughts. As I slurped my cone, I wandered down to the river bank and was absolutely shocked by its breadth and speed. The greenish water was racing by carrying countless tons of sediment from further upstream. I subsequently learned that at almost 2000 miles in length, it's the largest river in both the Yukon and Alaska, and drains an area larger than Texas. What I was seeing were only its upper reaches, but it was still colossal and impressive.

HAZY YUKON RIVER, NEAR CARMACKS

While I was finishing my ice cream, I met Sam from Rhode Island, riding a tidily-packed Honda CRF 250. Conversation with other riders (or anyone else for that matter) is easy enough when you're riding an older bike, especially when people notice the out-of-province (or territory) Ontario plate. It usually proceeds from 'what year is that' and expands from there. But even if you're not riding something out of the ordinary, conversations with other riders spring naturally from one's shared interests in bikes and travel and proceed from there. I've found many bike riders to be excellent company, often finding things in common well beyond the bikes and the road. Sam was one of those guys. We chatted agreeably for a while and as he knew the next fuel, a store and campground were at Pelly Crossing a little further up the road, we parted company with a loose arrangement to rendezvous there then assess our options.

By the time we got to Pelly Crossing our options were beginning to be limited. Evening was coming on quickly, the store would be closing soon and the next place offering any facilities was Dawson City, about three hours away. The municipal campground was on flat land next to the Pelly River and just across the road from the gas pumps. A few RVs and camper trucks were scattered about but it wasn't noisy or crowded and we quickly found a place for our tents.

Changing my worn rear tire for the knobbly was overdue. I wanted to retain what little life was left in the old one for emergencies, as I had no confidence that the knobbly would last well at all. I assumed the rough road surface on the Dempster Highway would rip it apart, and highway speed travel on the way home would finish it off. Oh yes, I forgot to mention the Dempster. Up to this point I had only been intending to ride as far as Dawson City to fulfil my promise to Jim, but Sam was planning to ride all the way to the Arctic Ocean at Tuktoyaktuk and had convinced me to at least ride as far as the Arctic Circle. I rather liked that idea, especially once I realized that the 'real Arctic' – the landscape of treeless plains and bare mountains – started not too many miles along the highway.

That evening, while Sam took a host of pictures with my camera, I changed the tires. Sam's first question was:

"You don't have a centre stand. How are you going to get the wheel off?"

"Like this" I said.

I had deliberately not filled the bike's fuel tank in Pelly Crossing before the store closed, noting that the pumps were self-serve as long as you had a credit card and I could delay it until morning, so when I didn't answer but just laid the bike over on its side, the panniers buffered with my big blue waterproof bag and the engine protected by resting on the crash bars, no fuel spilled. I disconnected the rear brake rod and undid the bolts which pinch the rear axle. I'll admit to the task being a little struggle, but having done it before in even less ideal circumstances, it was really rather straightforward. Eventually I had the rear wheel off, deflated the tire, liberally sprayed the rim with WD40 to lubricate it, and set too with the tire irons. The tires I use are far less difficult to remove and replace than most modern tubeless tires and it wasn't long before I had an undamaged tube in one hand and the rear wheel in the other. Putting the new tire on was slightly more tricky, but I've found that if you are careful and use plenty of lubricant it diminishes the chances of a pinched tube.

Getting the rear wheel assembled with the brake in the hub and the drive splines engaged properly and the axle back in place proved more difficult and I was happy to have Sam's help in lifting the bike so I could push the axle through. Eventually though, everything was back in

place and bolted up securely.

For the second night in a row I slept in the tent while my credit card stayed unused in my wallet. It had become expensive staying in motels every night but up until this point there had been few options. When I'm hiking I often tuck myself into some obscure corner and am gone before the world awakes, but it seems different when you have 500lbs of motorcycle to worry about. I suppose I could have found a spot or found a commercial campsite, but by the end of each day the former seemed like too much work and the latter was unappealing. Most commercial campsites are really RV parks – perhaps with a small patch of gravelly grass for a tent or two, a toilet block and showers – and are overpriced for what you get. At least motels gave me a chance to stay clean, stay in touch with family and friends and update my thread on the Adventure Rider on-line forum.

After manhandling the bike vertical again, Sam and I sat around chatting for a while. It was an oddly hazy evening. Smoke from distant wildfires was veiling the sun which resolutely refused to go down below the horizon. It was still light when we retired to our respective tents. At more than 62 degrees north, this First Nations community of Northern Tutchone people was still well south of the Arctic Circle but nobody seemed to have told the sun. I awoke in the small hours of the morning to wander over to the outhouse and it still wasn't really dark.

DAWSON CITY

By morning the haze had vanished and we awoke to clear skies. Sam and I rode most of the way to Dawson City together, only splitting up when I lingered to take some photographs of a wildfire burning on a distant hillside. His Honda rolled along nicely at just over 80kph – a speed he chose in the belief it would help preserve his tires and at which the Eldorado was barely breathing. He was easy to ride with, maintaining a steady speed, uphill or down, although I noticed his left foot was a lot busier than mine. On one stretch between photo stops, I noticed that he would make a couple of gear changes on the longer hills, whereas, once in 5th, I stayed there until we stopped again. Riding together or apart was fine either way, although I must admit I always prefer the latter.

I was fighting my bike. The new rear tire was arguing with the front over which would have the right to steer the bike. To say that it was disconcertingly squirmy for the first few miles is an understatement. The bike was almost uncontrollable and felt particularly unstable through corners. Fortunately, by the time we got to Dawson City, either I'd got used to it or the rubber had worn off those knobbly blocks enough that I ceased to notice its odd handling.

During the last few miles towards Dawson City the scale of past gold mining started to become clear. Vast heaps of river gravel lay in piles along the road – the abandoned detritus left by miners once the placer gold had been extracted by sluicing or dredging. I hadn't really thought much about the gold rush and the continued exploration for gold in the area, but it was clear that the activities were, and continue to be, on an industrial scale. Strangely, the gravel piles aren't unattractive, as they are composed of river cobbles from which the gold has been filtered, and not some abused, crushed and discarded industrial waste.

I'd been told I would like Dawson City. Because I work in the 'heritage' field, people often assume I'm interested in all historic sites and monuments, whereas I usually avoid them if I can and rarely visit museums or historical attractions. I was prepared for Dawson City to be a sort of Disneyfied Gold Rush World. To my astonished delight, it turned out to be nothing of the sort. Sure, there are shops and facilities geared to cleansing the wallets of the RV and bus crowd (and those of bike riders too), but the whole place has a real, living air to it. I spied a few folks in gold rush period costume but it was all very understated and unpretentious – unlike the dolt I saw standing on the pegs of his ADV bike on the main river road to impress that pretty blond girl.

I pulled up in front of a coffee house on the main street and had barely had time to order a coffee and muffin when Sam joined me. He'd seen my bike parked out front – well, it was hard to mistake – and swung in next to it. While we drank our coffees at a roadside table, I answered a barrage of questions from passers-by, some of whom recognized it as a Moto Guzzi and had stories to share, and others who wanted to know 'How old?', 'Who makes them?' (this one always annoys me as it says clearly on the tank), and, on seeing the licence plate (and with barely disguised incredulity) 'Did you ride this all the way from Ontario?' I began to feel like an exhibit at a sideshow, so as soon as we had finished our coffees I got up to depart. Just as we were leaving, the Harley-riding couple from Minnesota emerged from the shop. Once again, they looked a little surprised to see me; I wished them a safe ride. They were carrying on to Alaska; we were heading down the street to look for a room.

The 'Bunkhouse' is the de facto rider's rendezvous in Dawson City, mainly because it's the cheapest place in town to stay and is decidedly bike-friendly – the Swiss owner even providing free power-wash facilities to those who feel they need it. In common with almost every building in Dawson City, the bunkhouse is wood. It had balconies and stairways on all sides providing access to the many rooms. It stood out with its immaculate, flamboyant magenta and white paint job. The accommodations are basic: wooden bunks and a small wooden desk and chair. Toilets and showers are shared. While not cheap by southern Canada standards (a single room will cost you almost $100), it is clean, wholesome and welcoming.

On my first night in Dawson City, Rhode Island Sam and I split the cost of a room. I'd warned him I snored, a fact he had already ascertained for himself when we were camped at Pelly Crossing, so to soften the impact we walked down-town and I bought him a pair of ear-plugs before heading out for a drink. Afterwards he said he had slept well. I have no reason to doubt him, although the beer may have been as effective as the ear plugs.

The parking lot was full of bikes and Klim-clad riders were everywhere. There was the usual rank of BMW GSA 1200's, some virtually spotless, a scattering of Suzuki V-Stroms and two rather beaten-up BMW GS800's. I subsequently found out that one of the 800s belong to a Swiss rider who was making his way around the world, while the other belonged to Alaska Evan whom you'll meet a little later. The one bike that stood out like a sore thumb from all those ADV bikes – well, apart from my old Eldorado, of course – was an almost new KTM390, an orange and black praying mantis of a pocket rocket. This belonged to Aussie Sam, a long-time rider and sports bike fanatic from Australia. Abandoning his MVAugusta to storage in Melbourne, Sam had flown over to Canada, bought the KTM, and was making his way around the continent. When I talked to him, he was fresh back from Tuktoyaktuk. Somewhat to the dismay and amazement of the riders with their factory-prepared adventure bikes with their long travel suspension and knobbly tires, Sam had ridden his little rocket, with its street tires, all the way there and back without any problems at all.

It might have been a different story if the weather had turned bad. I've just finished reading another Dempster Highway trip account on the on-line ADV forum 'Adventure Rider'. A well-prepared, experienced rider from Wisconsin had been stopped by muddy road conditions between Eagle Plains and the Arctic Circle at the end of June. A day later the road was closed.

From the perspective of one's living room it's easy to imagine that 'a bit of mud wouldn't stop me'. But once you see how quickly dry, hard, shaly clay turns to unnavigable mush that clogs wheels, overheats engines and binds chains, it's a different story. I'm just glad I listened to the weather reports and turned south before there was the remotest chance of rain. My old Guzzi would have been a bit of a handful in anything but the best road conditions.

After getting organized in our miniscule room, Sam, Aussie Sam and I wandered the gravel streets and wooden boardwalks across town to the Downtown Hotel. I was expecting its Sourdough Saloon – home of the famous human toe 'Sourdough Cocktail' – to be a pretentious place where the cocktail was the focus of all activity. Instead I found a perfectly pleasant period bar, with plenty of seating, cheap beer, decent food at reasonable prices and friendly ungrasping waitresses. It was just a bar; an ordinary, agreeable place to have a drink with friends, eat a meal or chat with the many locals. Other than a small sign above the bar, the 'cocktail' was hardly noticeable.

Aussie Sam had one drink with us, then headed back to the bunkhouse for some rest. Sam and I lingered over a few more drinks while he waited for his laundry to finish. He had to keep running out to check on it, before we too headed back. This was the shortest riding day of my whole trip. It was a welcome break to relax and settle in early. The sun, predictably, was still high in the sky. It looked more like four in the afternoon than past eleven when I closed the curtains and went to sleep.

THE DEMPSTER HIGHWAY

I got an early start, leaving Dawson City while everyone else was sleeping. I love the mornings anyway, but who can sleep when there isn't any night to speak of. It's a twenty-five mile haul to the start of the Dempster, with nothing much to distinguish it, other than the 24 hour card-lock gas bar just out of town, where I topped off my fuel tank. The first few miles were nothing special – a well graded, hard-packed gravel road with a few areas of hard clay running between low hills clad in poplar, willow and spruce. The riding was easy, pleasant and stress-free. It didn't take too long before things began to become more interesting; the bush gradually became more stunted, the landscape more barren and the hills gave way to the bare and rugged peaks of the Tombstone Mountains. Exquisite.

Over many motorcycling trips I've tried to capture a bit of video footage, partly for my own enjoyment and partly to share with others on Youtube. Footage of droning along on the bike gets stale quickly, so I try to spice it up a little by recording the bike and rider in action against an attractive or interesting backdrop. The Tombstone Mountains certainly conformed to that criterion. I stopped the bike, dug my tripod out from the mess on the rear of the bike and set up the camera – actually two cameras – as I was able to perch one of my 'action' cameras on top of my digital, and capture the activity from two directions.

Once the cameras were in place and rolling, I got on the Eldorado and rode out of sight around a bend in the road before returning to ride past at normal speed. I did the same from the other direction, then returned to stop the cameras and pack up the gear. I had no idea whether I had captured anything useful (I did), but unless you try you have nothing.

Each time I stopped to play with the cameras, it ate up small bites of time; but how could I resist stopping to film a female moose and her two gangly, adorable young, grazing in a small pond just at the side of the road, or snap still after still of beautiful, bare-topped mountains rising from the swell of Arctic meadows? Ah, what scenery! You think it's spectacular, then you go a little further and it's even better. The rugged Tombstone Mountains gave way to the barren, rounded tops and talus slopes of the Ogilvie Mountains before the road entered the broad, rolling plateau of Eagle Plain. This is part of the unglaciated terrain which provided some of North America's first people with an access route into the heart of the continent from Beringia, the vast and now submerged 'land bridge' which connected North America to Asia when global water levels were much lower than they are today.

IN THE TOMBSTONE MOUNTAINS

While the mountains have a certain grandeur, it's the sheer scale of the landscape, the sense of isolation and the endless views which, for me at least, made this area so spectacular. As the Dempster Highway rises up the side of the Ogilvie Ridge it provided yet another a stunning view, this time across the Ogilvie River with the hazy mountains as a perfect backdrop.

Eventually Sam caught up with me. We chatted for a while and then we rode on separately again. His small trail bike was better suited to the unpaved Dempster than my lumbering Guzzi, and anyway, I was having far too much fun stopping and being flabbergasted by the scenery to hurry. Just a few miles south of Eagle Plains, I caught up with him. He had exhausted the contents of the Honda's small fuel tank and was in the process of adding some from his extra supply when I rolled up. I made some feeble joke about him having to be rescued, but it didn't really work as he was fully self-sufficient.

RHODE ISLAND SAM REFUELING

As we were riding the last few miles to Eagle Plains together, Jerry and Alaska Evan blasted past. I hadn't seen Jerry since he stalked me near Whitehorse and he gave a big recognition wave as he hurtled by in a barrage of dust.

From this point on we became a gang of four. Rhode Island Sam, Florida Jerry, Alaska Evan and me. Alaska Evan had just hopped across from Fairbanks and only had a few free days to nip up to Tuk and back on his BMW GS800. We were all solo travellers, all clearly quite comfortable in our own company, yet, without any deliberate plan, we had banded together in a loose association. After gassing up, we headed to the Eagle Plains dining room and sat down together without planning or thought. It was automatic.

The dining room was quite full. Many of the occupants were from a large cyclist group who were waiting for their accommodations to be sorted out so we were served relatively quickly. Jerry seemed rather taken with the eastern European waitress who was quite happy to chat, and we were all rather surprised at the quality of the food. Often such places dish up simple fare which, if one is being charitable, could be described as 'ordinary'. Our burgers were really good, and only a small bank loan was required to pay for them. OK, Nick, stop that! It's common to complain – or at the very least, be amazed – about the cost of things in remote northern locations until you start to think about the logistics, the distances and the overhead of providing even the most basic services. Fuel is expensive. I can't remember what we paid, but $1.60 per litre isn't unusual. But that fuel and whatever food we ate all had to be trucked in along the Dempster Highway from Dawson City – and Dawson City itself is a long way from anywhere else. So.....no more whining about expensive food and fuel – right?

After lunch Jerry and Evan rode off together, Sam rode on alone and I followed on behind. It was only another 22 miles to the Arctic Circle which had now become my destination. Why we attach meaning and significance to one place on the globe over another is for smarter people than me to philosophize over. At least, with the Arctic Circle, it's an indication that at 66 degrees 33 minutes you're well to the north. The Arctic Circle is the latitude at which, on the summer solstice, the sun doesn't set. But it's all smoke and mirrors. Because the earth's axial tilt fluctuates, the Arctic Circle isn't actually static, so the nice, clear sign-board where everyone stops to get their picture taken (me included), probably marks nothing of the sort. As of right now (according to our friends at Wikipedia), the Arctic Circle is actually racing north at a rate of about 15 metres per year. Close enough though. Let's not get caught up with semantics and mathematics which, I for one, don't understand.

As the four of us were fussing around taking pictures and shuffling bikes someone said,

'I don't see any circle'.

'Yes, there it is'. Sam joked, pointing a few hundred metres to the north of the sign. It wasn't the Arctic Circle of course – just a few linear patches of exposed bedrock which stretched across the landscape and which, if you used a little creativity and imagination, could be interpreted as a line. It was good enough for us.

I had been pondering my next move and my options were rather limited. The logical decision was to head back to Eagle Plains, sign into the campsite, then head south in the morning. But Eagle Plains was swamped with a large bicycle tour group who were slowly making their way from Tuktoyaktuk to Patagonia. They were travelling with support vans and endless equipment and more-or-less filled the campsite. I'd chatted briefly with some of the riders and concluded that even though many, if not most, of the riders were interesting people, the idea of riding back to join them wasn't appealing. Sam, Jerry and Evan were continuing north towards Tuktoyaktuk, intending to camp at a municipal campground at Fort McPherson. Sam was badgering me to continue north with them to Tuk. I think the idea of my unusual bike making it all the way to the end of the road appealed to him. But I had no intentions of going that far. I'd been watching the weather forecast which suggested rain within a day or two. There was no way that I wanted to be that far up the Dempster when conditions turned sloppy.

"Ride with us as far as Fort McPherson then', he suggested.

"It's only another 90 miles."

"OK".

Once again, the guys rode on ahead and left me to trundle along at my own speed. This was a good thing. The road crews had been out working over the previous days and the road looked immaculate. The trouble with immaculate gravel roads is that they are hell for motorcyclists. The grader had done a skillful job of smoothing the road, leaving an inch or more of fine-grade, unconsolidated, loose gravel on the top which concealed any underlying irregularities.

This made riding a bit tricky, especially on my old road bike. If I sped up, I was in danger of losing control as the front wheel had a mind of its own under the best of circumstances. If I went too slowly the bike would bog down in the deeper gravel or just wander. My tires didn't help. I had a mostly worn-out Duro on the front. It was never a success right from the start, didn't fit the rim evenly and bounced the whole bike at low speed on good pavement. On the rear was the Kenda knobbly I'd put on in Pelly Crossing with Sam.

The problem wasn't so much with the individual tires – it's that they both wanted to steer the bike and were in a constant battle for supremacy. I don't know if riders on more subtle bikes notice, but parts of the Klondike, Alaska and Cassiar Highways have longitudinal ridges and grooves which threw me around. It was generally OK, but once in a while one caught me out and the bike would lurch sideways unexpectedly.

Both I and the Eldorado have a lot of gravel road miles under our belts, so while the conditions were a little unpleasant, the worst part was that I had to focus on the road and couldn't let my eyes wander off across the landscape too much. I still hoped to see a grizzly (not too close) but had no time to let my eyes go lump-spotting across the broad Arctic meadows.

My mind, however, was free to wander. Some of the time it was plagued with Leonard Cohen songs which popped into my head unbidden. I'd be riding along in a meditative state when suddenly fragments from the album 'The Future', such as:

"Ah we're drinking and we're dancing

And the band is really happening

And the Johnny Walker wisdom running high"

would play over and over, so often and persistently that I began to wonder whether I was struck with some kind of seizure. When Leonard Cohen wasn't pestering me –

"And my very sweet companion

She's the angel of compassion

She's rubbing half the world against her thigh "

Stop it Leonard, please!

I thought about our little clan. Sam had suggested that after a few days most people want a little social contact, and what better than with a few like-minded folks who are all doing the same thing for similar reasons. He certainly put himself in that camp, happily admitting that he sought out like minded travellers to chat and travel with. I would add Jerry to that camp. He had basically hunted me down to make contact. At the time I wasn't sure how Evan felt. He kept his cards very close to his chest, but, in a subsequent message to me, he also admitted to seeking out contact while on the road. And me? I was happy to be hanging with such fine and pleasant folks. It's all a bit tribal. We have identified that others share our interests so we loosely associate for confirmation that we're not entirely daft, and perhaps, at some deep unspoken level, we know that there is at least someone close by to keep an eye out for us.

Sam was definitely keeping an eye out for me. I had stopped well before the Peel River and the primarily Gwich'in village of Fort McPherson. As you come over the last big rise, the vast expanse of the McKenzie Delta is spread out before you like a blue-green ocean. It was too stunning simply to ride by. Out came my camera. It felt like the edge of the world and a perfect place for me to end my northward journey.

When I eventually made it down to the ferry dock – basically just a bulldozed scrape down the riverbank to the water's edge – Sam was waiting, the other two having gone across on the previous ferry.

THE PEEL RIVER AND THE McKENZIE DELTA

Instead of going straight to the campsite, which was just inland from the ferry, Sam and I first rode on into Fort McPherson looking for some food. Like an idiot I hadn't thought about supplies and, although Sam offered to share his food, I opted to shop locally. The first shop we visited had a few bags of chips and some pop, but the owner generously phoned across town to a young woman who was operating a food truck to see if it was open. It was – the young woman, it turned out, was the sister-in-law of the first lady – and was happy to make me a burger and fries to go. Not needing a cooked supper, Sam returned to the campsite ahead of me.

While the food was cooking, I spent a delightful few minutes chatting with a group of young girls (some of whom were the daughters of the food truck lady) who had never seen so many cameras hanging off a bike, one of which was still running. They weren't in the slightest bit shy and were happy to talk with a dusty old bike guy and do a little acting up for the camera.

Evan, Sam and Jerry had already set up camp by the time I arrived. The campsite was really very nice. It was close to the ferry and had hot water (powered by a built-in generator), showers, flush toilets (oh, the luxury) and well-defined camping areas. We sat around chatting and drinking tea Jerry boiled up until the mosquitoes became too annoying and we headed for our tents. Even though it was about 11PM it felt like mid-afternoon.

FERRY ACROSS THE PEEL RIVER

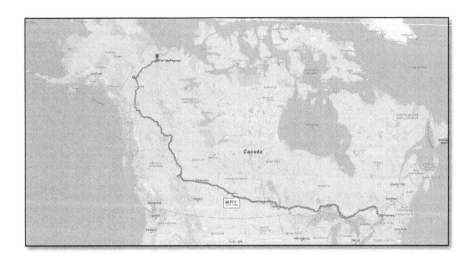

BACK TO DAWSON

The problem with being an early riser is I'm often up and ready for action long before it's useful or practical. That morning, for instance, I was up and organizing and packing my gear in my little one-person tent at 5.16AM. The ferry across the Peel River didn't start until 9AM, so I had the best part of four hours to kill. I spent some of that time catching up with my entries on my Adventure Rider thread, as I had no interest in feeding the hoards of mosquitos which descended whenever I poked my head outside the tent.

The other guys were continuing north to Inuvik and Tuk, but I was paying attention to the weather and didn't intend to be caught out on slippery, shaly clay on an old road bike – or any bike for that matter. Getting to the end of the road had never been an obsession for me. I'd seen the magnificent Mackenzie Valley Delta spreading out before me. That was good enough.

I don't expect everyone to share my attitude. Most people seemed eager to get to the end of the road – perhaps something to check off on a bucket list. I don't have a bucket list. I just like riding my old relic to distant places and seeing some interesting scenery.

By the time we'd got our bikes packed and said goodbyes, it was almost 9 and time for me to head down to the ferry. The ferry guys turned up promptly and set about doing their morning preparations and checks before waving me aboard. I've probably said it before, but I find the people in remote communities to be almost universally pleasant, friendly, chatty and hospitable. It's worth the effort of riding to out-of-the-way places for that reason alone.

When travelling in this land – or for that matter anywhere in North America – it's good to remember that we who are non-indigenous people are late-comers, spending a brief few moments on First Nations traditional lands where people have been living, often in extremely difficult and arduous conditions, for countless generations. These lands are the traditional territory of the Gwich'in people, who have lived in the area for thousands of years. They are still there, and likely to be for thousands more, so we outsiders should treat the area and its people with consideration. Tread lightly and with respect.

As the ferry closed on the Peel River's southern shore, an eagle was sitting just to the side of the road. I think it was an immature Bald Eagle (a mature one was just along the shore), although shortly thereafter I saw a pair which may have been Goldens. What a great way to start the day!

Riding south from Fort McPherson was a rewind of the trip up. As long as I made it back to Dawson City eventually, it didn't matter when.

The weather was still spectacular; there were clear skies, endless views, stunning crags and valleys and warm temperatures. The loose gravel was more compacted now as a few trucks had been by and hammered down a couple of tread-widths which, as long as I stuck to them and didn't veer into the loose stuff, made riding a lot easier. As before, I stopped multiple times to take photographs and fuss with my video cameras, and as before I was beguiled by the vast, open dramatic landscape.

I was conscious that it didn't always look or feel like this. While I rode along comfortably with all the vents in my jacket open and 20+c. air flooding into the tops of my leather chaps, I knew that such days were rare. The mean annual temperature at Eagle Plains is -6.5c. with winter conditions and below-zero average daily temperatures extending from October until May. Even in mid-summer, temperatures rarely exceeded 20c.

BACK INTO THE OGILVIE MOUNTAINS

As I wasn't following anyone, I set my own pace, taking time to enjoy the scenery from the return angle and take a few more pictures. At one point I stopped to have a close look at the deadly, black, shaly clay. Baked dry and hard it was easy to ride on at any speed, although the Eldorado still did a fine fandango every time she caught a rut. But those ruts showed me what a ghastly stuff it must be when it has been soaked. I could see individual wheel imprints, some of which dug an inch or two into the now-baked surface. Trying to grind a bike through that slippery slop would be dangerous and difficult work. I was glad I'd paid attention to the weather reports and got south before it got wet. The riding was fine, I was taking my time, riding at a sensible speed for bike and rider, and stops notwithstanding, I was making good time. It was the other vehicles that were giving me trouble.

The sun had baked all the moisture out of the road. Every vehicle larger than a motorbike trailed clouds of dusk in its wake. Because I'd been lingering over some scenic shots, I was soon caught by a transport truck, which must have crossed the Peel River on the ferry after mine. I'm fairly good about keeping an eye on my rear-view mirror, and spotted it while it was still a few hundred metres back.

"All the women tear their blouses off......"

Not now Leonard!

The truck was dragging a huge plume of dust. As he rapidly closed the gap between us, I put my indicator on to let him know I'd seen him, slowed right down, moved as far to the side of the road as I dared, and tried to memorize the road ahead. In an instant the truck blasted by and I was enveloped in the gravel dust. For what seemed like ten seconds, but was probably half that, I completely lost sight of the road. Eventually the plume thinned and I was able to find the road again, resume my position and gain back some speed.

My poor motorbike. The air filtration system on the Eldorado is, at best, primitive, and at worst, virtually non-existent. A rubber collar connects the two carb mouths to a box containing an automotive-style filter – one from old Austin Mini will fit. The trouble is the collar doesn't seal against the filter housing, but leaves large gaps where unfiltered air, or, as in this instance, fine particle gravel dust, can be sucked straight into the engine. I imagined all that abrasive dust grinding up and down the piston walls and getting trapped on the valve seats of my freshly rebuilt engine.

Other vehicles, RVs, trucks pulling trailers, pickups from either direction, created lesser plumes, but still stirred up the dust enough to momentarily obscure my vision and get between my teeth. I passed a couple of those ridiculous custom-made German and Dutch 'round-the-world', jacked up, 4WD, lion and bear proof Unimogs and Mercs. You have to wonder where they think they're going with those things, and that they must be deeply disappointed to find that most roads in North America are well paved. I suspect there is a profitable 'adventure vehicle' manufacturing industry in Europe, making and selling people expensive vehicles they don't really need.

I stopped in Eagle Plains only long enough to buy coffee and muffin, fuel up and chat with a couple of American riders who were parked outside. While we talked, a huge raven swooped down and stole a package of cookies that one of the riders had left on his pannier. It wasn't in the slightest bit shy and was soon back investigating a few crumbs that had fallen near the bikes.

On the way back to Dawson City I kept getting passed by those riders. They were mounted on V-Stroms, and were followed by a support van. They came blasting by a couple of times, gratuitously high on the pegs, the van far too close on the heels of the rear rider. Soon after, it was my turn to blast by (well, cruise by anyway). Their van had a gash in the side of its rear tire. Eventually the two riders passed me again – but I never did see the van. I passed one of the riders at the end of the Klondike Highway, and got to Dawson City well before them.

That night I once again got a room at the 'Bunkhouse', although this time I had the room entirely to myself. As I was retrieving a few things from the bike I met two recent arrivals, Scott and John from Iowa, who had just unloaded their bikes from the back of their van. Their spotless Suzuki DR650's were well-equipped with spare wheels and extra fuel tanks and were perfect for the ride they were planning up the Dempster Highway to Tuk.

Most riders who end up in Dawson City with plans to go further north have plenty of back-country riding experience which shows up as dents and dings on their bikes, worn footpegs, or (and this drives me nuts, I'm not sure why) a plethora of stickers on their panniers announcing how well-travelled they are. John and Scott's bikes could have just emerged from the crate, but that didn't matter – their enthusiasm was boundless and infectious. Through the miracle of Facebook, I subsequently found out that, after a weather-related delay, they did indeed make it to Tuk and home again without incident. Their FB posts respect and honour the First Nations people they encountered and stayed with, and their photos and comments are full of wonder and appreciation. The world needs more travellers like Scott and John.

ALASKA AND CASSIAR HIGHWAYS

Grinding back down the Alaska Highway the following day was an exercise in endurance. It's amazing how scenery that stunned and excited you one day can become so ho-hum the next – or perhaps that was a reflection of my mood. The day was punctuated by fuel stops. Fill up, run until almost empty or a fuel pump appears, repeat. I might have slipped a coffee or ice cream into the mix, but, basically, I just rode all day until I swung into a campsite near Teslin in the early evening. It was a super, quiet place, just a handful of small RVs and my tiny tent in a grassy field, until a young lady from Israel arrived and started to put up her tent. She wanted to make sure that everyone knew where she was from and that she was travelling on her own. She desperately wanted to engage anybody, everybody, in conversation. At the time I thought she was just annoying, although now I realize she was probably just lonely. I'm only slightly embarrassed to say I hid in my tent.

I retraced my ride almost to Watson Lake then headed down the Cassiar Highway. A number of people I'd spoken to raved about the Cassiar but, after almost two weeks on the road, I think I was at a low ebb and not really in the mood to appreciate it fully. My notes from the road say: "Nice road, fairly scenic, not as quiet as I had expected". Not exactly a glowing endorsement for one of the 'bucket list' motorcycling roads.

There wasn't much truck traffic but I saw plenty of bikes and far too many pestilential RVs. When I look back at my photos and video I see that the scenery is really rather grand, with mountains lining the route and plenty of lakes, ponds and rivers to add some scenic variety. Fresh from the wide-open world of the Arctic, perhaps I needed time to adjust to the world of forest-lined roads where stunning vistas only occurred through gaps in the vegetation.

ALONG THE CASSAIR HIGHWAY

When traveling on roads which traverse remote areas it becomes almost inevitable that you will end up at each of the little nodes of settlement along the way, since necessities like fuel, food and accommodation are only available in a very few places. By late afternoon my options were either to stay at Tatogga, carry on for another 90 miles to the lodge and gas station at Bell II or try for Meziadin Junction, 146 miles further south. I opted to stay put and spent the night at a motel in Tatogga, surrounded by Canadian Rangers who were off on an adventure into the mountains in the morning. It sounded like fun. They were planning to get dropped off on a remote lake by float plane, then hike into a cinder cone in the Mount Edziza volcanic complex. They were certainly keyed up for it. I was envious.

By this point in the trip, there was no question that I was on my way home and had started to smell the hay in the barn. This day's ride was between Tatogga on the Cassair Highway and Burns Lake on the road east towards Prince George. First though, I needed some breakfast.

On many days I didn't eat until lunchtime, but on this morning, I was famished by the time I got to Bell II. The Bell II Lodge was a lovely and impressive place, consisting of a huge log structure with a heli-pad, complete with two 'Lastfrontier heliskiing' helicopters ready and waiting to be used.

Bell II describes itself as 'A Northern Oasis' and 'A comfy full-service lodge' with log chalets, an RV park and camping, a restaurant and gas bar. With rooms ranging from $190 to $230 a night it was far too upscale for me and I was glad I'd stayed at Tatogga where the rates were more geared to budget travellers such as myself.

I parked the bike near the front door and wandered into the small side room hoping for coffee and at least something to stave off my hunger. Coffee was hot and fresh, and after draining my first cup I enquired whether refills were free (as they usually are in Canada), or if I had to go fishing for another $2.

"Help yourself", said the lady behind the counter. I think she was one of the owners.

"We have found people expect free refills and the extra income isn't worth the bother if we tried to charge for it".

The sign board on the wall offered two breakfast specials: a standard eggs/bacon/toast/homefries, or some kind of breakfast wrap. I went for the former. It was satisfactory, although could have been better for the $14 I was charged. Ooops, there I go again whining about costs in isolated places.

After my breakfast I walked outside where one of the helicopter pilots and his engineer were examining my bike. I was about to say 'admiring', but I'm not sure that would be strictly accurate. The pilot asked how the bike was running, and I truthfully answered that it was fine but a bit erratic – which was OK for the road, but perhaps not what one would like in a helicopter.

Just as I was pulling away, one of the helicopters lifted off and headed down the river valley, presumably to deliver or retrieve some hikers from a nearby mountain top. I like helicopters; they are noisy and they shouldn't really fly, but they sure are handy.

I spent the rest of the day droning along comfortably, eating up the miles. For much of the time the Cassiar Highway is lined with poplar and spruce growing close to the road edge, but every-so-often a magnificent vista of snow-topped mountains would appear through a break in the trees.

THE YELLOWHEAD

At Kitwanga I crossed the Skeena River – another colossal watercourse few people have ever heard of – and filled up again at the gas station at the junction of the Cassair and Yellowhead Highways. I didn't realize it at the time, but as I turned left on to the Yellowhead, I was joining the road I would be following for the next four days and 1600 miles, all the way to Winnipeg.

I thought about making the whole distance to Prince George but, as I was riding through Burns Lake, I saw a cheap-looking motel with a liquor store across the way. I was done for the day. After throwing some of my gear in my room, I wandered across the street............well, I would like to have wandered across the street, but in fact I had to skip across smartish as there was an endless parade of large, shiny pickup trucks coming around the corner far too quickly. It seems that unless you have a monster pickup in the West, you ain't no kind of a man.

I ducked into the mall, found the liquor store and bought a six pack of Okanagan Spring Porter. A nearby bakery was just about to close but was happy to sell me a cinnamon loaf dripping with syrup. I doubt whether my cardiologist would have been impressed, but I thought it made a fine supper.

I got back to my room just as three bikes pulled in next door and three obviously very well-heeled riders from Brazil ended their riding day. They were at the beginning of a mammoth trans-continental trip, having shipped their three new Yamahas (two ST's and a 660T) to Seattle (I think), planning to head up to Alaska, then down to Patagonia. My poor old Eldorado looked very dowdy and ragged next to their still spotless bikes with their shiny aluminum luggage. They probably thought I was poor and couldn't afford anything better. No doubt their bikes will acquire a little patina before they get too much further, although at this point their bikes, their riding gear – even the riders themselves – seemed to be of Teflon.

The following morning, I regretted polishing off the loaf and all six beer. Since my surgery a couple of years ago my tolerance for alcohol has diminished and six beers was about two too many, so it was a fuzzy Nick who headed east in the morning. Not far south and east of Burns Lake, the Yellowhead Highway parallels the valley of the Nechako River, essentially following it until it meets with the Fraser River at Prince George. I was unprepared for this part of British Columbia. I'd heard of the 'Northern Interior' but hadn't expected the mix of rich farmland, low rolling meadows, parkland and forest I saw between Fraser Lake and Prince George. It was a pleasant contrast to the mountains.

A few days earlier I had been contacted by an Adventure Rider forum member with the message that if I was passing through Prince George he'd like to meet. I must have been feeling uncharacteristically sociable because I agreed that if the timing worked out, we could meet for coffee or lunch. Well, we did. I was still feeling a little fragile, but a coffee, sandwich and conversation with Ray soon sorted that.

Many motorcycle people are excellent folks and Ray is certainly one of them. We chatted about bikes, travel etc. and he treated me to lunch (thanks Ray!). Then led me first to buy fuel and then through the town to set me on the best route east. One might expect such encounters to be awkward and the conversation difficult and stilted. Such was not the case. If we lived closer, I'm sure we could spend many happy hours chatting about our shared interests.

That evening I made it to McBride, dodging thunderstorms. I opted to stop early and pay an only slightly usurious amount for a room instead of the ridiculous prices quoted for motels anywhere near the touristy towns of Jasper or Hinton. My riding day was rather short. I was trying to kill a little time as the tires I'd ordered to be shipped to Jim's in Edmonton hadn't arrived on Friday and weren't going to materialize over

Eldorado to The Klondike

the weekend. I was hoping they would arrive on Monday; otherwise, well, I just didn't want to be hanging around Edmonton like a spare part for any longer than necessary. The irony was that the cheapo block-tread Duro I'd bought because it was the only 4x18 Alberta Cycle had in stock, was showing virtually no signs of wear and would almost certainly get me home. My front tire seemed unchanged. God knows what those tires are actually made of. I can't believe its rubber.

McBride lies in the Robson Valley surrounded by mountains. As I continued east the terrain became increasingly bumpy with patches of snow in the dark mountain crevices. I even noticed a small glacier in a cirque just above the town. I hadn't given much thought to the Rocky Mountains before, but they were starting to impress me with their size, rockiness and extent.

Leonard had deserted me. As I headed up towards Mount Robson, surrounded by towering snow-capped mountains, Joni Mitchell incongruously filled the void with random fragments:

"I met a redneck on a Grecian isle

Who did the goat dance very well

He gave me back my smile

But he kept my camera to sell"

Something, something about a rogue cooking omlettes...............Oh yes:

"And I might have stayed on with him there

But my heart cried out for you, California"

California? I thought she was a Canadian girl. What's she singing about California for? I guess Alberta didn't have the right number of syllables – or perhaps it was a marketing decision, with the lyrics changed by the music moguls.

There is no question that the Rocky Mountains are outstandingly beautiful with their classic peaks, their rocky cliffs and talus slopes and their tasteful spattering of snow, but while I was enjoying the scenery, it just wasn't exciting me in the same way that the open Arctic plains and mountains had.

THE ROCKIES NEAR JASPER

I moved on into Jasper, briefly stopped in a parking area along the main road, and was almost immediately in danger of being backed into by an RV whose driver hadn't bothered to check his mirrors. If I ruled the world, RVs of all descriptions would be instantly blasted into non-existence, along with guns and most buildings built after about 1930, and everyone would have to spend at least two years riding two-wheeled vehicles before they ever got close to driving a car.

Places like Jasper do this to me. Surrounded by beauty, they reel everyone in to spend too much money on stuff they don't really need or want. I couldn't get out of there fast enough.

My dour mood soon had additional fodder. Before reaching Jasper I'd stopped at a little lakeside pull-in at Yellowhead Lake for a brief rest, to snap a picture of the limestone cliffs above and to do a little mechanical tweaking. As I pulled back on to the road, I saw a massive elk bull grazing at the edge of the trees. I was deeply tempted to stop and take some pictures, but knew if I stopped, so would hoards of others.

Beyond Jasper the same scenario was in play. Similar elk – only this time the road was clogged with randomly stopped cars, their occupants desperately hanging out of the windows trying to get a clear shot. One stupid young woman had left her vehicle and was within 20 feet of the animal. She had no idea that this wild animal could trample or gore her on a whim. Meanwhile, traffic was slowing in both directions. If ever there were perfect conditions for an accident, these were they. I'm as eager and as thrilled to see wildlife as the next person, but not if it means putting others (or myself) at risk.

There was no point in me racing on into Edmonton in the morning as the mail was unlikely to be delivered first thing. To paraphrase Matthew (18:20), *'Whenever two or more are gathered together'*...............it's too many for me, so it's ironic that I was heading deep into darkest Edmonton for the second time on this trip. The last thing I really wanted was to be caught up in early morning commuter traffic as I headed into the city – but of course, I was. I'm not fond of cities. I had nothing particular against Edmonton, other than from what I've seen it looks like one gigantic box store complex, but once again I was taking advantage of Jim's skill, generosity, tools and workshop.

My trip across Edmonton was a rather harrowing experience, but I arrived at Jim's workshop, no thanks to yet more bucking and farting (the bike, not me). First things first, though. That oil, which had been cludging up the Eldorado's crankcase for far too long was soon gone, replaced by exactly three litres of Shell's finest Rotella. I don't think I've ever gone that far on one batch of oil and it had been weighing heavily on my mind. I had already bought the three new litres of oil the previous day and came very close to doing a quick and dirty roadside drain into the gravel, working on the principle that since a lot of oil comes out of Alberta, it only seems reasonable to return some. But in the end environmental consciousness won out.

The next job on the agenda was to fix my pannier which had started to sag after all the jolts and vibration from the Dempster Highway. The fibreglass boxes bolt to metal straps, the main one of which bolts directly to the frame. It's a poor design. After about 38 years one of the straps gave way and had to be welded. Now, after 47 years the second one has fractured in exactly the same spot, allowing the box to sag slightly. I had been supporting it with a couple of bungees.

Jim said, 'We could weld it,' and at first I thought he was joking. I should learn he's never joking. He's one of those guys that just gets stuff done. So, off with the bungees and the few remaining bolts holding the box to the bike. While I stood around redundantly, not only did Jim weld it, he reinforced it so it shouldn't ever happen again.

After that we – actually, he – soda-blasted the plugs until they were spotless while I cleaned and gapped the points and investigated the distributor wires, cap and rotor. All seemed fine, although, when I pulled the wires, the brass end for the No. 2 cylinder where it enters the cap, was badly corroded. We didn't understand this as they were new wires from the last time I was sponging in Jim's garage.

Not surprisingly, when I cleaned it up and put everything back together, the bike started and idled as the manufacturers intended. Well, to be honest, it might be a little noisier than they intended, but it sounds good to me.

With all the major tasks completed and the bike running well, Jim went back to do some office work while I lounged in a dentist's chair, surrounded by interesting motorbikes and spotless tools, waiting for the mailman and catching up on some email.

While I'd been on the road I'd checked in with Florida Jerry and received some sad news. His V-Strom had run low on oil by the time they reached Tuk and had damaged something in the engine. I was curious to know how he was faring, so from the comfort of Jim's chair I dropped him a note. His reply was almost instant. He was fine, and astonishingly, he too was in Edmonton. I didn't get any details but it was good to hear he was safe. He had even rented a car to do a bit of sight-seeing while he sorted out the logistics of retrieving the bike.

Well, the postman duly arrived at the normal time (about 12.30) bearing my two new Duros. I hastily loaded them on the back of the bike, said my goodbyes and thanks to Jim and was soon fighting midday traffic on the Yellowhead through Edmonton. Fortunately, that didn't last long, and with the bike running nicely we were humming East.

Lest I'm giving you the impression that pounding up to the Arctic circle and beyond, then back through the mountains of BC and Alberta on a 47 year old bike is a walk in the park, let me itemize a few of the 'issues' I encountered. I've told you about the raggedy low speed running. Despite the replacement carbs and proper set-up, it continued to be rough at low speed. I wondered if the bob-weight springs in the distributor were worn out, although since the distributor cap moves around at will, that, too, could be part of the problem. These hiccups only occurred at or near idle and most of the time the bike was running perfectly at highway speed. (*Note: I eventually found the source of all these poor running issues – stay tuned. Info below*).

The horn had vibrated itself loose somewhere in Saskatchewan on the way west and despite bolting it back in place hadn't worked since. It may have been banging around by its wires for an age before I'd noticed. And I hadn't had a rear light since.......I don't know when. The rear light fitting was worn out so the bulb couldn't connect properly. I did eventually manage to get the rear and brake lights working for most of the journey home.

Slightly more worrying were issues with the gearbox and the clutch. As the miles accumulated, upshifting continued to be fine and smooth, but downshifting became clunky, with neutral becoming increasingly hard to find. The clutch was starting to drag, especially while sitting in traffic after a long run.

That knobbly rear tire droned noisily and, with the cylinders sitting out there in the breeze, the tappet clatter is always audible. But...it sounded the same when I set off and continued to run happily at a steady 60mph hour after hour. As long as I had my earplugs in properly, all was serene.

One temporary fix involved a pair of channel-lock pliers and some copper wire. I'd had just about enough of the popping and backfiring on deceleration - goodness, it's not a Harley – and I have Guzzi's dignity to uphold. For ages, the right-side exhaust pipe had been leaking where it joins the cylinder head. In their wisdom, Guzzi used a threaded collar that pulls the pipe into the head where a flange near the end of the pipe is supposed to seal against a round copper gasket. As you tighten the thread to get a seal, the gasket deforms, eventually turning flat and ineffective. After handing over some cash to Canadian Tire, I wound a few rounds of copper wire between the flange and the pipe end, carefully inserted and locked down the pipe.....and magic, no more leaks.

You may be asking yourself why any sane person would put themselves through an enormous trip, limping along from one Heath Robinson fix to the next. The short answer is, I enjoy it. It adds a little challenge to what would otherwise be just another long ride. Occasionally I did find myself looking wistfully at immaculate full-dress cruisers as they glided effortlessly by (especially while I was doing yet another roadside tweak), but then I would turn the key, the old Eldorado would fire up again sounding almost as it should, I'd throw my leg across, settle into my well-worn seat, clunk into a gear and ride off happy.

And then I was back on the road, heading east along the four-lane Yellowhead Highway through flat farmland, the mountains a distant memory. There's not much good one can say for that kind of riding, other than you make time. With four wide lanes most of the time, it's a stress-less and fast way to get across the prairies. At first, the weather was fine and, as I looked out across those endless expanses, it once again dawned on me that the prairies are rather enchanting. There's nothing spectacular, and even things of note are few and far between, but there's an awesomeness to the scale of the land and sky that has its own kind of magic. I stopped a couple of times to try and capture something of the grandeur landscape, but it would take a more skillful photographer than me.

I crossed the prairies in two hops, staying in Saskatoon the first night after leaving Edmonton, and Portage La Prairie the second. I had hoped to go further the second day, but I encountered a little delay. Let me elaborate. As you know, the Eldorado had been misfiring from time to time especially at low speed. I'm tempted to say 'since time immemorial' but she does run well most of the time, despite the record here. This never really bothered me and, although I fiddled with her from time to time, I didn't really pay much attention, since a dirty plug, some sparking at the points – a multitude of things can cause a misfire and they often clear themselves. But then, in the middle of Manitoba, far from any settlement, she died, with the empty whirring of pistons rushing up and down cylinders with no spark to power them. I hastily pulled over to the side and started a good look around.

THIS IS SUPPOSED TO ATTACH TO THE COIL

I must admit, I'd been wondering about the coil for a while. It lies underneath the fuel tank. When I looked under the tank I could see that the lead, connecting the coil to the distributor, had come loose and the connector, which was supposed to be attached to the coil, had rotted off. There was hardly anything left of the connector post. Darn unreliable Guzzi. Substandard Bosch parts. The coil had only been sitting there, quietly doing its job for over 100,000 miles and 47 years. It was hard to be too upset, although it was decidedly an inconvenience.

I dug out my tools. There was no space to fiddle with it without removing the tank, which meant removing the seat etc. Arghhh. And even if I got at it, there was no guarantee that I could do anything with it. That terminal was all but gone. I looked west. I'd been running ahead of a massive grey-black thundercloud. It was fast approaching.

Just then a Harley roared by, geared down, turned around and joined me.

"You OK?" said bearded Bill (I'll call him Bill - I didn't catch his name).

"Yes. Thanks for stopping, but I think I've got everything I need"

EVERYONE CARRIES A SPARE COIL, DON'T THEY?

As he'd been slowing to join me, I'd suddenly remembered the old coil in my bag of bits on the inside of the fairing. Assuming it was still good (and I'd never checked it) I could just unhook the wires from the under-tank one, find a temporary place for the new one, and carry on.

After a bit of fussing around and connecting the wires to the wrong places a couple of times, I Gorilla-taped the coil to the bike's side panel, turned the key, and miracle of miracles, the old Eldo roared to life. Rarely have I been so happy. That monster thundercloud was getting really close. But my glee was short-lived. As I rode on, I noticed that the alternator light on the dash was now permanently on. Darn it - had I fried my alternator?

I rode the few miles to Portage La Prairie, where previously I'd had no intention of staying, booked into a motel conveniently next door to Canadian Tire and pondered my options. How far can a guy ride just on the battery even if he turns the lights off? Not far enough, was my guess. What if I bought a spare Lawn Tractor battery (yes, that's what's in the Eldo already)? How far would that take me? Again, I concluded, only far enough to get really stuck.

During that evening, to the entertainment of some of the other motel guests, I did a more robust fix for the new coil and cruised the internet for any suggestions or help. I found one ray of hope. On the Scramblercycle web site (from whence I'd bought the alternator kit) there was a reference to some circumstances where the light would stay on even though the alternator continued to charge. OK, I thought, I'll hang around until Canadian Tire is open in the morning and see if I can get someone to check my battery/alternator with a multi-meter.

As I sat killing time in Tim's the next morning, I did some more Googling about testing alternators. According to some folks, with the bike running, if you detach the battery ground wire and the bike continues to run, your alternator is good. I gave it a try. Not only did the bike continue to run, the revs actually dropped a little as I reattached the ground — indicating draw on the alternator. Whoopee!!!

THE LONG ROAD HOME

Rolling along across the prairies, I was once again struck by their size and the surprising, subtle differences one could detect from one part to the next. I loved the Ukrainian churches I passed. Their Byzantine-influenced architecture seemed oddly suited to the vast, open plains and formed an interesting counterpoint to the massive grain elevators and farm silos which dotted the landscape. However, as I suggested on the way west, such sights were few and far between, the road itself was undeniably dull and I was beginning to long for some entertainment beyond the half-remembered fragments of songs in my own head.

During a spring motorcycle trip to Quebec, I'd experimented with a Bluetooth headset which linked to the music on my phone. It worked very well for hearing turn-by-turn directions from Google maps while riding through towns, but was virtually useless once I was riding at normal road speeds. There was just too much wind and engine noise entering my helmet to make listening to music enjoyable. Actually, it was all but inaudible unless I had the volume cranked up fully – and then it just descended into too much noise.

Perhaps I was better off with Leonard and Joni. Joni was just then reminding me that:

"The wind is in from Africa

Last night I couldn't sleep"

The wind was actually behind me for a change. After the headwinds of the journey west, I was delighted to be pushed along. It had the marvelous effect of quietening the engine noise, diminishing the wind roar and stretching each litre of fuel to the maximum. Perhaps I should have brought that headset along after all.

I skirted around the south of Winnipeg on the bypass and was soon heading towards the Ontario border. The countryside had changed again. Rich fields extending off into the far distance had given way to scrub forest of spruce, poplar and tamarack. I was humming quietly to myself:

"My fingernails are filthy

I've got beach tar on my feet"

when I noticed some bikes closing fast behind me. Four big modern bikes: a Goldwing, a Victory – I can't recall the others – steamed by in the fast lane with a look and a wave. Twenty minutes later I pulled into a service station to refuel to find the bikes parked and the riders making their way to the pumps to look at my, by now, rather bizarre looking Guzzi. They could hardly have missed the two tires bungeed on the back, and it didn't take them long to notice the coil strapped to the side of the bike, the gravel dust congealed in oozed oil on the engine and the dusty Ontario licence plate.

"Where are you heading?" one of the riders asked.

"I'm on my way home to near Kingston," I replied.

"Where have you come from?"

I couldn't resist a bit of a smirk as I said,

"The Yukon and the Arctic Circle."

I know – pompous git – but at least it was the truth.

The riders headed inside for lunch while I continued on my way. I saw them again briefly again in Dryden a couple of hours later as I was just leaving after a late lunch and they were stopping for a mid-afternoon coffee. One of the guys said something about not being able to keep up with me, but we were working from a different set of priorities. I was heading home, while they were out for a gentle cruise around Lake Superior. I wished them safe riding and carried on. After a five hundred mile day, I stopped for the night in Nipigon. Despite the warning light staying on and rain for most of the second half of the day, the alternator had continued to charge the battery and power the lights, the coil had unfailingly provided sparks and I wasn't stuck at the side of the road in some desolate spot. That was a result I could be happy with.

The skies were heavy when I left Nipigon but the bike was still holding together, I had a full tank of fuel and I was riding a road I liked. The Lake Superior coastal route may not have the jaw-dropping scenery of the Rockies or the sense of remoteness of the Ogilvie and Richardson Mountains along the Dempster but it does have a magnificence that is entirely its own.

I wasn't too far along before I saw a Harley stopped at the side of the road. I slowed, then pulled up just as a large white SUV arrived facing the rider. I assumed it was a local work crew looking to see if they could help – then I noticed the dark uniforms of the two occupants and the piece of paper being handed to the rider.

"Do you need gas?" I called out.

The rider indicated that he didn't and I got out of there before the police became too interested in me.

Sometime later I was stopped at the rear of a line of vehicles at a roadworks traffic light when the Harley rider rode up alongside. Using language that I won't repeat here, and which, of course, would never pass my lips, he explained that he'd just been given a $375 speeding ticket for 139kph in a 90kph zone. I'm not sure I'd ever believed that a Harley would go that fast before but here was the evidence. The rider had all kinds of excuses to explain why his speeding was completely justified – something to do with following a truck that was getting his nice pants dirty. He clearly had no sense that the road was anything but his personal racetrack.

As the light changed and the traffic started forwards he moved right up behind the other vehicles, blipping his throttle (loud pipes, of course) making a total prat of himself. As soon as there was any space, he raced by all the other vehicles and disappeared to his pressing appointment with an ambulance or the police. I have no antipathy towards Harleys. Some are fine, even vaguely interesting motorbikes (in the same way that Ford F150s are interesting), and I have met some excellent people riding them, but this jerk confirmed all the stereotypes.

When I posted a note about this incident on the Adventure Rider forum, one guy responded that the 139kph he was charged with was suspiciously close to 50 kilometres over the posted 90kph speed limit. He suggested that the police were actually being kind. They could probably have charged him with 'street racing' and impounded his bike.

After the haul along the northern part of Lake Superior, most people stop to refuel in Wawa and many people stop for a coffee at Tim's. I did too. It was crowded, so I stayed just long enough to gulp down my coffee, contact my son Alex, who was working at Pancake Bay Provincial Park, and head south.

Not far out of Wawa I came across another bike at the side of the road. This time I just slowed doing the thumbs up/thumbs down signal to check whether everything was all right. It was, so I carried on. An hour or so later, I had pulled over to remove my rain jacket when a Yamaha FJR purred up behind me and the same rider proffered the same hand signals. We both had a good laugh over that.

I headed south along the lake shore, stopped briefly to say hello to my son in the park and almost as soon as I left, the rain started. This was not just any rain. The skies over Batchewana Bay were heavy with thunder clouds and I ran right into them. There was little to do but tuck down behind the windscreen and carry on. Many cars had their four-way flashers on and the road was awash with water in seconds. Astonishingly, although the coil was sitting on the side panel exposed to the worst of the rain, the bike didn't falter during the deluge. Only later, just east of Iron Bridge, once the rain had settled into a less biblical downpour, did the Guzzi splutter and eventually die. A quick spray with WD40 and we were soon running again.

PENULTIMATE NIGHT - FIXES AT KEN'S

Eventually I arrived at Ken's place. My fix of the exhaust leak had done stirling duty since Edmonton but, as these things often do, it had reappeared, so the Guzzi was back-firing and spluttering as I arrived in Webbwood. It was oddly appropriate as, if you remember, I'd left with the bike misbehaving too.

We tried to repair the exhaust and managed to block most of the exhaust gases from escaping at the cylinder head but it had become clear that the threads in the head needed some loving care and that anything we did now would only work for a while.

I had just one more day to ride before I slept in my own bed.

THOSE BIKE WOES

In all my descriptions of the various problems that I encountered on the road, I haven't talked much about the clutch. Back when Yves was putting my engine back together after replacing the pistons, cylinders and oil pump and I was there to pick it up, he picked up the clutch intermediate plate (it's a three plate, car-like dry clutch) and said he didn't like the look of how it was showing wear.

"Oh that will be fine." I said (or something to that effect).

"It was working well before. Just bolt it up."

So he did.

To cut a long and dreary story a bit shorter, as the miles went by the clutch increasingly started to give me trouble. Most of the time it didn't matter. Riding across Canada involves hours when you don't ever have to touch the clutch or gear lever. Get it into fifth and just cruise. Problems only arose through towns or while stopping for the interminable road works.

At first all was fine. Gear changes could be a bit clunky, but it's a Guzzi, so nothing new there. Eventually though, it became difficult to find neutral at a standstill. Wait — I'll rephrase that — it became impossible to find neutral at a standstill, so I had to make sure I was down through the gears and into neutral before coming to a complete stop. This is all very well for the occasional road-works, but through Edmonton morning traffic it was a nightmare. I hadn't mentioned it to Jim — he'd have wanted to rip the clutch out right then.

To compound these issues, the clutch had become more of a light switch than a rheostat. It had two positions: on and mostly on. If I pulled the lever to the bars it would disengage the engine, but if I sat for more than a few seconds, the bike would start to move forwards without any input from me. This was a trifle disconcerting.........

But......with careful management it got me home, and honestly, I only have my cavalier attitude to mechanical stuff to blame. It's certainly not a Guzzi problem. The clutch has been excellent and reliable over many miles.

Then there were the brakes. Did I mention the brakes? I thought not. Some things are best left unsaid until you're safely back in your own domain and the bike is parked in the garage.

The Eldorado has drum brakes. Stop rolling your eyes now – they are actually pretty good when they are properly set up, especially the four leading-shoe front brake which can be quite effective. When I left home, the brakes were working well. The rear came on softly and predictably and was strong enough to lock the rear wheel with only a moderate amount of pedal pressure. The front was a bit more aggressive. The first part of a lever squeeze didn't do much but pull a little further and the front of the bike would start to dive and progress would slow rapidly. I'm not talking about twin-disc braking power here, but certainly enough to safely slow the bike.

When Rhode Island Sam and I changed the rear tire at the Pelly Crossing campground, this meant removing the rear drum, as it's built into the rear hub. Once the tire was changed and the wheel was back on the bike, I adjusted the brake rod and assumed it would be fine. Not so! There was far too much travel at the pedal and what little braking there was was pathetic. I gave the adjuster screw on the brake rod a few more turns which brought the pedal resistance to where it should be, but had little effect to increase its power. Perhaps I'd been a bit too liberal in my application of WD40 to the tire and wheel parts. Perhaps I'd got some of that slippy silicone liquid on the brake shoe. Oh well, it will wear off eventually, I thought, especially when a bit of gravel dust from the Dempster makes its way in there. That, at least, was my logic.

It never did improve. A soft rear brake is not a bad thing when riding on dust and gravel so I barely gave it another thought. As for the front brake, if it had become a bit grabby and that didn't bother me either. Using too much front brake on gravel is a sure recipe for landing on your ear.

On the way home I 'managed' the brakes. By keeping my distance from other vehicles, staying alert and aware of the road conditions and traffic around me (when there was any at all), I could slow the bike using the gears (see above) and rely on the brakes for those last few yards to get me stopped. Easy on the front brake though. I won't pretend it was always easy, and it did cross my mind that I'd be in serious trouble if I ever needed to do an emergency stop,

Management of deficiencies seems to be what riding old bikes is all about. I grew up on a host of bargain-basement two wheelers with raggedy cables, useless brakes and worn out tires, so learning to accommodate problems became second-nature. By the time I was back in Ontario, the Eldorado had become more or less unridable – at least by most people's standards; dragging clutch, minimal brakes, noisy exhaust – but we struggled on, putting in some decently long days through inclement weather. Looking back on it, a wise person would have at least taken the time to adjust the brakes properly, but when you're close to home after a long trip, wisdom doesn't always take first place.

Over the last few miles, back on extremely familiar roads, I gave myself a talking to.

"You know Nick, most accidents happen close to home. People get careless."

I deliberately slowed down, watched other road users, looked for people emerging from driveways and side roads and obeyed all the speed limits. After many untroubled and accident free days and so many miles, it would have been stupid to crash close to one's own front door.

At 6PM I rolled into my driveway, shut off the engine (before it disturbed the neighbours), gave the old girl a pat and walked into the house.

I was home.

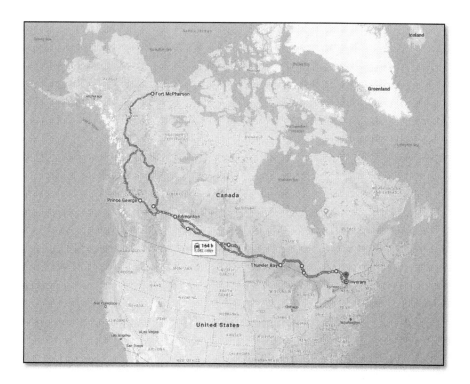

A few facts and figures:

GOING OUT
Inverary On to Webbwood: 673kms (418 miles)
Webbwood to Terrace Bay: 705kms (438 miles)
Terrace Bay to Rennie MB : 782kms (485 miles)
Rennie to Roblin: 556kms (345 miles)
Roblin to Viking AB: 796kms (474 miles)
Viking to Edson: 337kms: (209 miles) (included stop in Edmonton)
Edson to Pink Mountain BC: 769kms (477 miles)
Pink Mountain to Watson Lake YT: 742kms (461 miles)
Watson Lake to Pelly Crossing: 719kms (446 miles)
Pelly Crossing to Dawson City: 250 kms (155 miles)
Dawson City to Fort McPherson NWT: 587kms (364 miles, 340 unpaved)
Fort McPherson to Dawson City YT: 587kms (364 miles, 340 unpaved)

COMING BACK
Dawson City to Teslin: 708kms (439 miles)
Teslin to Tatogga BC: 568kms (353 miles)
Tatogga to Burns Lake: 646kms (401 miles)
Burns Lake to McBride: 436kms (270 miles)
McBride to Spruce Grove AB: 501 kms (311miles)
Spruce Grove to Saskatoon SK: 550 (341 miles) (included stop in Edmonton)
Saskatoon to Portage la Prairie MB: 695kms (432 miles)
Portage la Prairie to Nipigon ON: 890kms (553 miles)
Nipigon to Webbwood: 811kms (503 miles)
Webbwood to HOME: 673kms (418 miles)

22 days, 13,981 kms, 8687 miles.

(PS. These mileages are derived from Google Maps. Actual mileages are probably slightly higher - not that is matters at all).

PART 2

ACROSS LABRADOR ON A SCOOTER? ARE YOU MAD?

A fourteen-year-old scooter may not seem the logical first choice for a bike to ride from Ontario to Newfoundland, then back across Labrador, especially since I had far more suitable bikes in my garage, so a little explanation is in order.

After owning more than a hundred bikes and riding many hundreds of thousands of road miles, my friend Norm had started riding a Suzuki Burgman 650, finding it answered all his needs. With plenty of speed and comfort and almost endless storage space, it, or one like it – he still swaps bikes like underwear – found a permanent place in his garage. Despite numerous offers, I'd spent ages ducking his suggestion that I try his scooter. I'd had scooters in the distant past. Like many motorcyclists, I had a negative attitude to what I thought of as small-wheeled, underpowered, commuter vehicles for the elderly, fit for trolling along in the slow-lane, and not much more. Then I broke down and rode it. What a revelation. It was fast, it was comfortable, it had great brakes, the engine was turbine quiet and electric motor smooth, and although the handling took a little getting used to, it could be hustled around corners quickly.

My wife Chris has ridden on the back of most of my bikes and is a confident and skilled passenger, but we have always found the accommodations cramped; fine for a short rides, but not suitable for long distance tours. As her knees gradually deteriorated, she was finding getting across the seat and into position was increasingly difficult. Norm suggested we give the Burgman a try. By sliding a leg through the low step-over in front of the driver's seat, Chris was able to slide on to the front seat, then move back on to the passenger seat with relative ease. Once there, she found the high rear seat allowed her to see more of the road. She's never liked looking at the back of my head.

After a few local rides, we found the Burgman to be a wonderful two-up bike. The broad plush seats are comfortable, the bike has more than enough power, even when heavily loaded, and, best of all, we have acres of space. I can barely even feel she's on the back. It was time for an adventure.

TO NEWFOUNDLAND

The previous year we'd driven by car to Newfoundland and spent time exploring Gros Morne and the western side of the island and loved it. When you look at a map, Newfoundland doesn't seem very big. It's just an off-shore island stuck out there in the Atlantic. Unless you study the map scale you get little idea of just how huge it is. We had intended to explore the west coast, then zoom over to the east to romp around there, but we quickly changed plans once we'd experienced the scale of things, promising ourselves that we would return again.

This time we opted to take the scooter. We thought it would be the ideal vehicle for touring around to the enormous list of outports, early settlements and museums that Chris had identified as 'must see' places. I like long distance rides and will happily sit on a bike for ten or twelve hours a day, only stopping for fuel and the occasional bite to eat. Oddly, Chris doesn't see the fun in this; she chose to fly and spend a few days exploring St. John's, while I rode the bike (notice I've stopped referring to it as a scooter).

It's a long haul from near Kingston, Ontario, to St. John's, Newfoundland. Over the previous weeks I'd packed and unpacked numerous times, getting the organization of things just right. The tent, one sleeping bag, a sleeping pad, tool roll, tire repair goo and sundry other things filled the cavernous space beneath the seats. Our clothes and the second sleeping bag filled the Nelson Rigg soft panniers I'd slung over the rear, while Chris's helmet and riding gear filled the top-box. She only took hand luggage on the plane with the rest of her stuff on the bike.

DAY 1: Inverary, Ont. to Fredericton NB. (1122 kms (697 miles))

"You take that thing on the highway?" I heard questions like that, or observed expressions, which suggested the same thing many times over the following few weeks. The answer, of course, was a categorical "You bet!" Leaving home at shortly after 5AM, I headed straight for Ontario Highway 401, riding west towards Montreal. The Burgman transmission is super-slick. As you pull on to the on-ramp and open the throttle, the revs rise and the bike charges up to highway speed in a flash. No really – it does! I had rented a Suzuki V-Strom 650 in the UK earlier in the year and I found the Burgman to be every bit as fast and possibly a little faster, as no time is wasted changing gears.

I soon settled in at ambient traffic speed. This equated to between 120 and 130kph (74-80mph), at which speed the Burgman's engine was humming nicely at about 4500 rpm – far below the 8500rpm red line. There were numerous large trucks on the road at that hour, generally governed to around 110 kph, so I passed many. I got a perverse pleasure from seeing the surprise on many drivers faces as they realized they were being overtaken by a scooter.

Beyond the Quebec border, I crossed the St. Lawrence River at Salaberry-du-Valleyfield, skirted Montreal then headed along Quebec Highways 30 and 20. These are long boring highways with little to recommend them other than being quick ways to move through the countryside. Instead of following 20 all the way to Riviere-do-Loup, I took a scenic detour along Highway 289, which parallels the international border, rejoining the Trans-Canada Highway at Edmunston, New Brunswick. It's a testament to the comfort and relaxation of riding the Burgman that, although I'd already ridden 849kms (527 miles) by that point, another 273kms (169 miles) to Fredericton seemed like nothing much at all. I checked in to a motel and slept well.

DAY 2: Fredericton, NB to North Sydney, NS. (638kms (396 miles)

I had completely overestimated the time it would take me to get from Fredericton to the ferry dock at North Sydney, Nova Scotia, so I arrived with far too many hours to kill. I was so early, in fact, that I couldn't even park the bike in the ferry parking area. My boat didn't leave until 11.45PM and the earliest I could put the bike in the line-up was 6PM. It didn't take long to exhaust the attractions of North Sydney. Once I'd filled the bike and taken a couple of strolls around the town, there was little else to do but pull out a sleeping pad and lie down for a snooze.

Eventually hunger got the better of me so I drifted over to Tim Hortons for a bowl of chili, meeting a couple of local riders in the parking lot, who pointed me to a short, scenic loop which would help kill some time.

By the time I got back, I was able to get inside the ferry dock gate and I spent the remaining dreary hours hanging around the ferry terminal, being studiously ignored by the 'real' riders on their decked-out Harleys.

DAY 3: Ferry to Port aux Basque, Port aux Basque to St. John's (7hrs ferry + 904 kms) (561 miles)

In the belly of the beast, the deck hands pointed to straps hanging along the side of the vessel and left me to it. Despite its bodywork, the Burgman was not as difficult to strap down as I anticipated. It has some substantial hand-rails and these became my main points from which to strap to the divots in the deck. I added a second set of straps to the lower fork legs. These were more marginal, but at least kept the bike from shifting if the seas got rough (they didn't).

I've taken this ferry before and usually any attempt to sleep is interrupted by people talking with no concern for the well-being of those around them. This time it was different. Many people almost immediately eschewed the lounge chairs, opting to sleep on the floor. I did too. I'd brought a sleeping bag and my ear plugs up from the vehicle deck, and, while I can't say the passage was entirely restful, I did manage to get a little sleep.

The various two-wheelers on board were some of the last to disembark, trailing a lengthy parade of vehicles all heading in the same direction along the Trans-Canada Highway. As soon as I could, I pulled off, partly to give the line of traffic a chance to sort itself out, and partly to put on my rain pants and jacket as the morning air was chilly and damp.

Crossing Newfoundland is a lengthy trip. Mine was punctuated by the need to stop every 250 kilometres (155 miles) to fill up with fuel.

The Burgman only has a 15 litre (3.3 Imp. Gals, 3.9 US Gals.) tank and by 200 kilometres the dash light would be starting to nag me insistently. Usually I was able to combine pee or food stops with refueling, but on longish rides, the need to fill up occurred with irritating frequency.

It was well towards evening when I hit the outskirts of St. John's, dialed Memorial University into my phone for directions and worked my way through town to the residences where Chris was staying.

DAY 4 to DAY 15: NEWFOUNDLAND

This report is about riding the scooter across Labrador – I'll get there eventually if you just hang in there, and I don't intend to bore you with a day-by-day account of our holiday together. Suffice it to say that other than the first day, when we visited Signal Hill and Cape Spear and it rained hard all day, we had a wonderful time and the weather was acceptable. The Burgman was an absolute delight to travel on.

It proved easy for Chris to get on and off, was comfortable and easy to manage, and provided us with that sense of 'being in the landscape' that you simply don't get when you travel by car.

We worked our way around the Irish Loop, explored the Avalon and Bonavista peninsulas, visited historic sites, watched endless seabirds, wandered around scenic villages, chatted to locals and generally had an exceptionally good time. If anyone is thinking that they might enjoy a visit to Newfoundland, don't hesitate. It really is wonderful.

Long before we were sated, it was time for Chris to fly home again and for me to make the long ride back.

DAY 16: St. John's to Plum Point

Chris's flight was scheduled for late afternoon, but she's a big girl, perfectly capable of looking after herself, so I left early in the morning for the other side of the province. Long before we had started the trip, I had been pondering the idea of taking the long way home through Labrador. It would add a few more days, and, of course, I would be riding what some would view as a totally unsuitable vehicle, but that made it all the more intriguing. I wouldn't be the first to ride a scooter on the Trans-Labrador Highway but it would be interesting to see how it (and I) fared.

Day 16 was wet. That's a bit of an understatement. Virtually the whole time I was riding – all 914kms (568 miles)- was through heavy rain, rain, road spray, and during the more pleasant bits, drizzle. Despite being well protected by many layers, by the time I got to the motel in Plum Point, just a short hop south of the ferry to Labrador, I was cold and wet to the skin. I've yet to find any combination of rain gear that can withstand persistent and unrelenting soaking. Perhaps some of the new, high tech rain suits are impenetrable, but I doubt it, and anyway neither my budget nor sense of aesthetics lends itself to the full Power Ranger get-up.

After a change of clothes and a shower (not necessarily in that order), I wandered down to the bar for some food and a couple of beers, falling into conversation with the only other guy in the cavernous room. I learned a lot about fishing the Straits of Belle Isle that night, most of which has now evaporated.

DAY 17: Ferry: St. Barbe to Blanc Sablon + Blanc Sablon to Happy Valley (619kms) (385 miles)

I was at the ferry dock ridiculously early, having left my room shortly before 5AM to ride the few remaining miles from the Plum Point motel. I hadn't booked my passage in advance and wanted to be at the head of the line for a place on the 25% of the space they don't book. You never can tell how many people are going to be wanting to cross, and I was eager to make sure I got on the first boat. I needn't have worried. Only a handful of people turned up without prior booking and there was plenty of space available.

Once I had my ticket, I moved the bike down to the loading area. While I sat enjoying the morning air a fellow from North Dakota ambled over to chat. Once we'd dispensed with the 'Did you ride that all the way from Ontario' conversation (He'd noticed the Ontario licence plate), and I explained that it really wasn't the little scooter he was imagining, we got along fine. He and his wife had been travelling in a medium-sized RV, towing his wife's spotless new Audi – 'Her baby' as he described it. They had left the RV in Newfoundland and brought the Audi on to the ferry to explore the Labrador coast.

I told him that as far as I could remember, paved road extended from Blanc Sablon to Red Bay. Beyond that the road was being paved at an alarming rate, and he could anticipate some gravel sections and roadworks anywhere north of Red Bay.

The ferry takes about an hour and forty-five minutes. The crew have unloading down to a fine art and I was soon riding past the line-up of cars, trucks and bikes waiting to board. I must admit to chuckling quietly to myself when I saw a small group of ADV bikes, decked out with extra sets of tires and God knows what else. I didn't notice whether they looked my way – probably not.

Almost as soon as I turned on to the main road up the coast the road turned to mush. Where there had been rough but serviceable pavement was now a horrid mess of chewed up asphalt, gravel and grooves, all turned to a nasty slurry by the recent rains. As I rode along letting the Burgman's front wheel find its own skittery path, the wet gravel dust spraying over the bike, I thought about the lady's poor Audi. I'm guessing they didn't get very far in Labrador. Fortunately, the road works were patchy, separated by long paved segments. Not that I really cared. Chris and I had already experienced our share of potholed gravel roads in Newfoundland, and even two-up the Burgman had acquitted itself admirably. I had no real anxieties about the long sections of unpaved road which I knew awaited me.

When I'd ridden the Trans-Lab in 2010, the stretch from Red Bay to Port Hope-Simpson had been a narrow, rough, red-gravel road clustered with potholes. It had actually been one of my favourite stretches of the whole route. It felt wild, remote, challenging and perhaps a little dangerous. Now, almost perfect pavement wound its way across the landscape, dramatically reducing the effect. Such was the perfection of the asphalt that there was a real temptation to speed. However, with no trees to slow it, the wind whipped across the tuckamore in erratic gusts, convincing me that maintaining a moderate speed was in my best interests. It's still a nice road to ride, but much of that sense of adventure has been lost – at least for me.

At Port Hope-Simpson the road turns inland away from the Labrador coast. Virtually the whole stretch between Port H-S and the junction with the Cartwright Road (516) was under construction. At the time I was riding most parts had a broad gravel bed – the final stage of road preparation before paving. This was all very well, but it made a truly horrible surface for riding. The top inch of gravel was loose over a firm bed. I kept my speed down and concentrated on letting the scooter slither around wherever it wanted to go, only giving it a little throttle when things really started to get interesting. When road conditions are like this, you have to focus on staying relaxed and upright. As soon as you start to clench up, trouble arrives.

By good fortune, no trouble appeared and beyond the Cartwright turn-off the road reverted to being a normal northern Canada dirt and gravel road with hard-packed sections, some loose bits and plenty of potholes. Riding slowly on the loose gravel had eaten up plenty of time so I plugged along, only stopping infrequently to take the occasional picture, relieve myself or add some fuel to the bike from my spare can. The section between gas stations is 410 kilometres (254 miles) so the extra 15 litres of fuel I was carrying gave me some breathing room.

HEADING INLAND FROM PORT HOPE-SIMPSON

By the time I hit the tarmac again, about 90 kilometres south of Happy Valley/Goose Bay, it was well into evening and starting to cool down. And by the time I got to the bridge across the Churchill River, I was both tired and cold.

Everyone who rides this route comments on the bridge. Whoever designed and welded the bridge base must have wished motorcyclists an unpleasant death. Riding across on my old Guzzi had been bad enough. The metal grid would grab the tires and jerk you around. On the scooter, with its smaller wheels, it was diabolical. The bike was wrenched from side to side in a most disconcerting and unpredictable way. It felt as though the bike was being thrown feet in either direction. In reality it was probably just inches, but it was very unsettling.

Eventually I made it into Happy Valley, found the only available room – a luxury suite at an eye-watering price. I was too tired to argue and not interested in looking to see if there was anything else available, so I just bit the bullet and settled in for the night. I was too late and too tired to even find a beer.

99

DAY 18: Happy Valley to Manic-Cinq (900 kms) (559 miles)

Even though my luxury suite came with the promise of a breakfast buffet, I couldn't be bothered to wait until they opened so I headed up the road to Tim Hortons coffee shop. I'd broken one of my cardinal road rules – always fill up with fuel the night before – and was now stuck until one of the town's gas stations opened. As I sat over a coffee and doughnut I chatted with some of the other patrons, answering the usual queries about the scooter. It is always interesting to see the looks of disbelief when I tell people that I've registered over 100mph on the speedo and that it will cruise all day at 80. Eventually I asked one of the guys which gas station would be open first, and he said,

"You'd better ask Jim here – he'll be opening up soon".

Jim (not his real name of course – I've long ago forgotten it) was sitting nursing a coffee, but very generously swigged it back, got me to follow him down the road behind his 4-wheeler. Within a few minutes he had the pumps turned on and was able to fill the bike and the spare tanks. I headed west towards Churchill Falls and Labrador City.

Back in 2010, the only paved parts were short segments at either end of the highway. All the rest was gravel and dirt. Now it is all paved – a perfect ribbon of tarmac stretching right across the heart of Labrador. Once again, the immaculate road surface is an inducement to speed although I kept my throttle hand under control, partly because I'd heard horror stories of dozens of people getting speeding tickets (the road has an 80kph limit), and partly because a strong head wind made riding fast just too much hard work, even hiding behind the Burgman's enormous screen.

There is no denying that the nature and scale of Labrador is awesome and that alone is reason enough to make the trip. The road goes on and on through stunted spruce, past endless swamps, across numerous rivers and streams and across massive glacial boulder fields. In places, forest fires have burned the landscape for as far as the eye can see. The Burgman hummed along as I fell into my usual habit of featuring artistic productions in my head, this time playing the 'Lord of the Rings' movie while my lizard brain took care of riding the bike. Most of the time there were no other vehicles in front or behind, but somewhere east of Churchill Falls a Jeep had crept up behind, then sat, matching my speed at respectful distance. After about half an hour I needed a nature break and pulled off into a flat gravel area, which must have once been a construction staging yard. To my surprise, the Jeep immediately pulled in too, its driver jumping out to ask 'Whatever kind of scooter is that?' After following me for so long, he just had to find out what manner of scootery beast could maintain those speeds with such apparent ease.

It's a good job I had the 'Lord of the Rings' on my personal, internal DVD as I was beginning to find the Trans-Lab a bit ho-hum. When you are riding gravel roads you have to pay attention all the time just to stay upright. With the gravel now buried beneath the tarmac, the perfect road unwinds before you. You are far more of an observer than an active participant. You are disconnected from the landscape through which you are passing. It is like being in a video game. You might just as well be in a car.

I briefly pulled into Churchill Falls to refuel, then headed back on the highway, reaching Labrador City by mid-afternoon.

Apart from the paving which had changed the Trans-Lab dramatically, the other change which I couldn't help noticing was the massive hydro corridor which now parallels the road for most of its route. There had always been a powerline near the road, but in the last few years this has morphed into a 100 metre wide scar across the landscape with two parallel lines of metal support towers marching like giants from hilltop to hilltop. While the road swings around lakes, swamps and knolls, the powerline takes a straighter course, crossing the road from time to time. I understand that such things are necessary if we want to run our toasters and power our electric cars, but damn, do they have to be so ugly?

It was Saturday, and as I closed in on Labrador City I noticed that there were other bikes on the road, their riders enjoying the opportunity for a weekend ride. I saw a couple of Harleys, a pair on an older Goldwing, and an older airhead BMW with a full fairing. It must feel a bit stultifying to live in a town with only one paved road to ride, but if you have the bug, you have to ride, even if your choices of road and destination are limited.

I pulled into the Shell gas station on Avalon Drive and filled my tanks before heading out to the Tims on the hill at the edge of town. I hadn't eaten since breakfast, and with many more miles to ride, needed to stoke up. Tims chili is a robust meal for the price. I'm always a bit suspicious that it may have been lingering in the heating pot for weeks, but so far, I've eaten it with no ill effects. When I had arrived at Tims mine was the only bike in the parking lot, but as I walked towards the scooter it was no longer alone. Two bikes – a Victory and a Harley – were parked next to mine and the three folks in motorcycle gear I'd noticed inside, were standing chatting.

"Sorry," I said, "I hadn't realized this was the <u>real</u> motorbike parking area."

They laughed. If you live in Labrador City, you know that if someone arrives on a bike they will have ridden hundreds of miles on gravel, since there is only the one road in and out, and there are long gravel sections in each direction. My dust covered scooter looked dowdy and travel-worn compared to their immaculate cruisers.

"What size engine is in that thing?", one of the riders asked (the '650' badge was covered by my bags) and was quite surprised to hear that it was a 650. He was thinking a 150, or perhaps a 200. We chatted for a while about this and that – typical motorbike roadside talk – then got going on road conditions. There is about 12 miles of paved road south of Labrador City before you hit the dirt near the Fermont mine and the road starts to crisscross with the railway. When I'd driven this section in an SUV last year the road was in truly horrible condition: sloppy, rutted, potholed and dangerous. I was dreading it on the scooter so I asked them about it. To my great relief they said the road was in excellent condition: hard-packed, well graded, and treated with calcium chloride to keep the dust down. And they were right. It was in wonderful condition, with only a few short areas where fresh gravel had been graded over the hard-pack.

Coming gingerly around a corner on one of the looser sections, I found a rider parked at the side of the road and swung over to see whether he was OK. Of course he was; he was just taking a short break before the last little section to Lab City. I'm lousy with names so I'll call him Jakub. Jakub was a young man – perhaps in his late 20's – from the Czech Republic. He had been on the road in North America for months and was fresh back from Alaska. He described this trip as his big adventure. He told me that soon he would have to settle down, become a family man and become responsible. I did my best to convince him that he didn't have to give up on life and excitement just because he was starting to get a bit older. The two are not mutually exclusive.

His V-Strom was festooned with stickers from his travels and looked every inch as though it had seen some real adventures. It was tatty, scruffy and probably hadn't been cleaned in months. While we chatted Jakub kept looking at the Burgman.

"We have those in the Czech Republic", he said, in that annoying perfect English so many Europeans manage.

"But nobody would think to take them on journeys like this. Perhaps to the seaside once a year...".

About 40 miles south of Labrador City (don't quote me on this – these are approximations), the paving started all over again and continued all the way to Relais Gabriel – the first fuel source to the south. I had been thinking about stopping nearby, either to camp or in the accommodations at Relais, but there was still light, I had full tanks of fuel and I had energy to burn. I pulled back onto to Highway 389 and continued south.

Between Relais Gabriel and Manic Cinq the road is mainly decent, hard-packed gravel. In my not-so-humble opinion this is some of the finest riding on the TLH. There is great scenery of high forested hills, frequent glimpses of Lac Manicouagen in the distance, plenty of bends and creek crossings – an engaging road with lots to keep the mind alive. Be warned though. There were many places where the road has been 'improved'. It is changing fast and who knows how long it will be before it too becomes just another paved road through the Quebec bush.

By the time I got to Manic-Cinq, it was almost 9PM, the light was gone, and I was thankful for the excellent Burgman headlights which had made nighttime riding a pleasure. As the light had faded, I had flipped up my visor and ridden along with my face exposed to the fresh air. There were no insects to bother me and few vehicles to stir the dust. Without the visor I had an unimpeded view of the road ahead. I skirted around the edge of the massive Manic-Cinq dam which looked ghostly and bizarre, the individual bays illuminated from below. I swung into the rest stop/gas station/motel. The restaurant was closed, but a room was available, there were some interesting beers on sale, and there were three channels of fuzzy French TV. I settled in for the night.

DAY 19: Manic-Cinq to Home (1167 kms) (725 miles)

I'm one of those guys who'll wave at anyone riding in the breeze whether they're on a motorbike, scooter, trike, Spider, four-wheeler, mobility scooter or lawn tractor – I'm an equal opportunity waver. I figure that if you're out there moving through the fresh air, it's all the same game and we're all having fun. I draw the line at side-by-sides though, they are a step too far removed from motorcycling. And I'll chat to anyone, even if I personally find their choice of steed bizarre or uninteresting and it's a struggle to find anything mannerly to say about it.

When I arrived at Manic-Cinq, I pulled up in front of my room. Two bikes, BMWs – a K1600 and a smaller one I didn't recognize – were parked next door, the two middle-aged male owners standing close by talking. It's one thing not wanting to engage in conversation – I respect anyone's right to keep to themselves – but these two prats consciously and deliberately avoided even the slightest indication that they were aware of my existence and cut me dead, even going as far as to turn away so they wouldn't have to engage. When I left Manic-Cinq at around 5AM, I'd wished I'd been on one of my noisy Guzzis. I would have wheeled it close to their window and revved it up before leaving. They deserved it. The Burgman is so whisper quiet, so I doubt they were even aware that I'd left.

The road is all paved from Manic-Cinq south to Baie Comeau. It is a lovely road – a bit rough in spots but wonderfully twisty, scenic and fun. Unfortunately, the road engineers are working fanatically to ruin it. Work was already in progress to straighten out corners and broaden the road-bed. Even in the half-light of morning I could see where sections of bush had been measured and cut for new sections of road, and machinery was already in place to start removing rock and soil. It must be a terrible road along which to navigate a large transport truck, and I do understand the necessity of changing roads to suit their evolving uses, but darn it – another fine motorcycling road is about to be forever diminished. Within a year or two it will be just another big road from which to gaze at a big world through your windscreen.

HIGHWAY 389 SOUTH OF MANIC-5

After fueling up once again, in Baie Comeau, I headed west for the long haul home. At the last light as I was leaving town, two Harleys pulled out ahead of me, and once past the built-up area, sped to well above the 90kph limit. I suppose I should know better at my advanced age, and shouldn't play games with people's egos, but I pulled up behind them and matched their speed. I could see them eyeing me in their mirrors. They sped up. I matched their speed again until they were rolling along far in excess of the speed limit. I figured that as locals they probably had a handle on what was permissible, and if we attracted the attention of the police they would be at least as likely to get a tickets as me. Eventually they moderated their speed to about 20kph over the posted limit and I allowed them a little breathing space, settling in a few hundred metres to their rear, trailing them for 120 miles, all the way to Tadoussac.

A few miles west of the ferry at Tadoussac it started to rain and didn't really stop until near the Ontario border. Once again, the rain eventually worked its way through my clothing until I could feel dampness next to my skin. My leather gloves were completely sodden, but I found if I turned the Burgman's heated grips on, my hands stayed comfortably warm. Usually I will do almost anything not to have to ride through Montreal. This time, though, I just followed the signs and worked my way through the city without major hold-up or incident. That it was Sunday probably helped. Traffic densities were nowhere near what one would expect to encounter on a week-day.

Once into Ontario, I continued plugging along, sitting between an indicated 115 and 120kph. At one point, a group of riders on a variety of bikes, went past in the fast lane, travelling smoothly and comfortably at about 130, the lone woman on a Harley waving as they passed. I briefly thought about tagging along but decided that after eleven or twelve hours in the saddle, I was tired and it would be wiser to stay at moderate speeds and ride alone.

By putting in long days, it only took a single day longer to ride home from St. John's via Labrador. Admittedly, these were long days. I didn't spend any time sight-seeing and barely stopped, other than for fuel for me and the bike, and to take the very occasional photograph.

You might presume that, with its small wheels, the scooter would be a bit of a handful on the long gravel sections. I found it to be perfectly stable and predictable. Perhaps, if I'd been riding some ADV machine I could have ridden those sections a little faster, but this was more than offset by the general level of comfort the Burgman provided. My backside never complained, my legs stayed flexible and my back was fine.

I'm not suggesting that everyone rush out and buy a scooter for long distance rides and gravel roads. What I am suggesting is that the large scooters are excellent travelling companions, more than capable of multi-day, multi-mile rides to anywhere you fancy. In the final analysis, the Burgman will not replace any of my old Guzzis. They will always remain my first choice for long rides. There is an indefinable quality about the way they move me that can't be replaced by mere efficiency and capability. Nevertheless, while I don't think I will ever warm to the Burgman in the same way, its ability to carry two large people two-up in comfort, its long-distance reliability and ease of handling won it my respect.

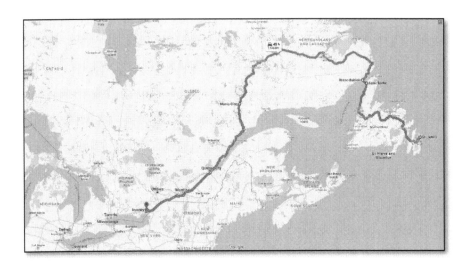

PART 3
CONVERT TRAVELS

FIRST RIDES OF THE YEAR

There is something special about the first few rides of the New Year. Once Ontario winter hits, the opportunities for riding vaporize as snow and cold cloak the world for three or four months. Getting back on the bike again once the roads are ice and snow free and the temperatures aren't killing-cold is always a special delight.

But getting the bikes anywhere near the road is the first problem. My driveway stupidly slopes down towards my garage. As the warming sun melts the snow, the run-off flows towards the garage door then freezes again over night, leaving a solid mass of clear ice which extends half way across the garage floor. For years now I've been intending to address the issue, but I always forget about it once the warmer weather arrives. Digging the bikes out of two inches of hard ice then wheeling them up a slippery incline isn't an enticing way to start the riding season. I've dropped bikes on more than one occasion and it's always a struggle. Is it worth it? Oh yes! Once all the gear is on and the bike is running up to road speed, all the irritations and frustrations melt away.

My first ride is almost always the same: twenty miles north to the gas station in Westport to fill the tank, then twenty miles south again before hypothermia sets in. If it's two or three degrees above freezing and the sun is shining, I might extend the ride for a few miles and make a loop, but I have to stick to well-travelled roads where salt and traffic have done their work and no patches of compacted ice remain. Whichever route I take, there's plenty to occupy the mind and keep the eyes engaged.

There is something rather wonderful about riding a bare, dry road with snow-banks to either side, ice on all the lakes and snow lying like a blanket in field and forest. With spring on its way, there is life in the willows and dogwoods. Deer and turkeys are no longer hiding in the deep forest, but are out and about, browsing on twig ends or scratching through the snow for the residue of last year's corn harvest.

On this, my third ride of the year, I wait until after 10AM for the thermometer to crawl past freezing. The light snow of the past couple of days has left some damp patches in the shadows and I want to be sure that no ice will surprise me. At first, my Moto Guzzi Convert is reluctant to start. It's been a while since I charged the battery, and it has lost most of its charge in the cold garage. It cranked over slowly and the engine popped and wheezed a couple of times before refusing to turn over any more. Fortunately, my USB battery pack was fully charged and, once connected, cranked the engine easily.

The Convert is an automatic. When it's running at a fast idle on the choke, the torque converter engages and the bike wants to move forward. I hold it on the rear brake, noticing that the pedal is a bit soggy, and make a mental note to myself to drain, refill and bleed the brakes before too much more time has past. Once the engine has warmed up a fraction, I walk the bike forwards across the sheet of ice and out into the sunshine. I'm swaddled in multiple layers, my helmet is in place, my scarf is pulled up across my nose, and my silk liners and winter gloves are on. I walk over to the bike and hit the starter again. This time it shudders to life quickly, and I'm soon able to drop the choke levers and pull away.

The chill wind quickly finds its way through any tiny openings in my clothing, whistling in under my visor and making my eyes water. I don't care. The roar of the bike and the feel of the road beneath my wheels are seductive and glorious. Even when the temperature is below freezing, the late winter sun is often strong enough to start melting the snow, so I take it easy, drifting along at a mellow 50mph until I'm away from the farm lands and into the more rugged world of rocks, trees and water which starts a few miles north of my home. The road seems fine, but it pays to be vigilant. It's disconcerting to be riding along on a dry surface, then suddenly encounter a broad strip of running water extending right across the road – usually on a corner or in the shadow of a cliff. Black ice can lurk in these dark places. I do a quick mirror check to make sure no one is on my tail, cut my speed, then cross at ninety degrees with the bike vertical. I do any leaning before or after the wet spot. Even though I'm well-padded with multiple layers of clothing, I have no desire to go sliding down the road on my side.

After a few miles the creeping cold in my fingers and toes reminds me that there is more to life than always being warm and comfortable. Two of my bikes have heated grips, and while I appreciate and use them when they are there, I have no desire or interest in adding them to the Convert. With central heating in our houses, and with cars with heaters, heated seats, and, God-help-us, heated steering wheels, we have become disconnected from and unused to the slightest amount of discomfort in any part of our lives. Plug-in jackets, heated socks and thermostatically-controlled gloves allow us to take living room levels of comfort to the motorcycle road. Some bikes even have heated seats. I eschew them all. I want to feel those sharp darts of chill wind piercing the gap between my jacket sleeves and my gloves. I welcome the creeping cold which stiffens my knees and makes me wiggle my toes in my thick winter boots to keep the blood moving. I feel wonderful. Perhaps the heart surgery I went through a couple of years ago has sharpened my focus. While sitting in my chair at home, I often find myself absent-mindedly fingering the wires which lie just below the skin and which helped to hold my sternum together. They, and the nine-inch scar down my chest, are a permanent reminder of how fleeting and transient is human life. Others may wish to insulate themselves from discomfort; I relish it as part of the experience of being fully alive.

The road winds on past frozen lake and rocky forest, the low sun casting long tree shadows across the still deep snow. The snowbanks lining the road are filthy with a winter's worth of salt, sand and road grime, but in the bush and on the lakes it is still pristine. I pass a narrows between two lakes, where open, flowing water has started to eat away at the edges of the ice sheet. Swans and Canada Geese have found the opening and are feeding, heads down in the frigid water. In a few weeks the Ospreys and red-winged blackbirds will return too.

The Convert's exhaust is suddenly loud as it reverberates back at me from the iron safety barriers, jarring me from my daydream and reminding me that I'm balancing on 500lbs of hot metal. Reaching a straight section, I twist the throttle, the revs rise, and the torque converter works to catch up as the bike surges forward. It is not a fast bike, but 70mph arrives quickly enough, and, apart from more cold wind, doesn't feel much different to 50. Since I'm well over the speed limit, I throttle back to more moderate, and less chill-inducing speeds.

I reach Westport, quickly flip the cap to see plenty of fuel sloshing about, and ride on past the gas station without stopping. I know from past trips that I can easily cover 200 miles on a full tank and I'm only about 50 miles into this one. With a population of only about 700, Westport isn't much of a metropolis and I'm soon through and climbing the steep slope up the Maberly Road. All the land to the south is a wedge of relatively low-lying Paleozoic sandstones, conglomerates and glacial till, while to the north, a massive block of Precambrian gneiss and marble rises above the village and forms the north shore of both Wolfe and Upper Rideau Lakes. The impressive Rideau Lakes Fault, up which I was climbing, is an ancient fracture in the earth's crust and marks the edge of the Algonquin Highlands – which would have been quite impressive had the last glacial ice sheets not ground them almost flat.

There isn't much traffic on the Maberly Road, especially in late March, and other than a propane truck out on delivery to some rural homesteads, I have the road almost entirely to myself. Indeed, during the whole 33 mile stretch to my next destination, I see only three or four vehicles. The Convert wafts along in a most satisfying way. I control my speed almost entirely with the throttle, only rarely needing the brakes for the few tighter corners. Although it is still chilly, the sun has some warmth and my body has reached equilibrium with the air temperature. I no longer feel cold; even my fingers and toes are comfortable.

There's noticeably more snow in the bush north of Highway 7. I pass a neat line of snow machines, freshly parked from a blast through the woods. I suspect their owners are inside the adjacent bungalow, enjoying a mid-morning post-ride beer. A little while later I roll past a farm entrance, garnering astonished looks from two men working on a truck.

I decide I'm not quite daft enough to turn down my unpaved shortcut to Wheeler's Pancake House – my lunchtime destination – opting for the longer paved loop through McIntosh Mills. In the summer the shortcut is a pleasant, narrow, hard-packed gravel and dirt bush road. At this time of year though, the sun will have melted the upper inch or two of the road-surface into gravelly soup, except in the shadows, where snow and ice will linger.

The road that leads to Wheeler's is surprisingly busy; their parking lot is jammed with cars and people are milling around the entrance to the massive log eating-hall. I usually head to Wheeler's during the week when there are rarely more than a handful of others around, so I'm shocked to see it so busy. Then I remember – it's Sunday, and the first sunny day of spring when the sap will be running. I wheel the bike around and head away.

Hunger has started to eat away at me so I pull into the Tim Hortons in Perth, order a bowl of chili from the busy and flustered counter staff and settle into a seat near the window. An old guy starts chatting to me about the winter road conditions, but as we chat, I realize that he's probably about my age. I like to think I'm wearing my years well but am still surprised by the strangely familiar geezer looking back at me in the bathroom mirror. After a few minutes I notice another motorbike in the parking lot and we are joined by its leather clad rider who informs me that he rides year-round. His bike is a heavily modified Honda Rebel, blacked-out and bobbed for winter riding. We share a few riding conditions horror stories for a while until I take my leave and head for home.

My route takes me along a delightful winding road where the winter sand lies deep in the corners and patches of punky snow remain in the shadows. A few die-hard ice fishermen are still out on the lakes, but the recent rains have turned the top surface grey and, even though I know there's still at least a foot of ice, it looks unstable and I wouldn't risk it. I ride with care, navigating around the tricky spots, but with no traffic to worry about, I can choose whatever cornering line I like, making it back to the highway without a single slip.

The temperature has gradually been rising throughout the ride and, while the sun has only briefly shown between the thin clouds, the air is warmer and my fingers and toes are no longer chilled. I pull back into my driveway. The warmer air has turned the upper surface of the gravel to mush but has done little to melt the ice sheets by the door. I turn the bike around and paddle it back into the garage, ready for a forward start the next time the roads are clear and the weather obliges. I can't count on that being tomorrow, the day after, or even next week, but winter is gradually releasing its hold and these early-season rides are driving away the winter blues.

SPRING RIDE TO SAGUENAY

On each ride there is always something that dominates the senses. Sometimes it's sound: the roar of the wind around the sides of the helmet, the contented hum of the engine, or in the case of my Moto Guzzis, the clackety-clack of the tappets. Occasionally it's the way your bike and body interact that sets the tone for the ride. Wind buffeting, vibration, the jolting of the bike over road irregularities and bodily aches and discomforts may take the upper-most position in your consciousness. Of course, one's eyes are always active, scanning the road ahead for hazards, catching the flutter of a wing in the treetops or a movement in the grass where a deer decided to turn tail, rather than play Russian roulette with the traffic.

During this trip, smell overwhelmed my other senses. It will remain what I remember most about the ride, long after the delightful hours of riding on quiet roads beside rivers and lakes and through snow covered hills, and the less delightful time spent doused in spray from heavy traffic on the four-lane highway, have faded into a distant memory. You see, it's spring, and spring can be odoriferous.

As I made my way across rural eastern Ontario it seemed as though every farmer along the route was fertilizing his fields with a whole winter's worth of accumulated animal droppings. The fields were crawling with muck spreaders, flailing their stinky loads across the flat terrain. And where no equipment was to be seen, the dark stained soil and the heavy smell of sewage hit my nostrils and showed that the farmers had already been active. Some fields reeked of cow manure, others of pig or chicken – the latter so acrid it almost made my eyes water. I can't say I really minded though – it's all part of the seasonal pattern of farming life, renewal and crop growth. Before too long, those brown stinky fields will be head-high with corn stalks or knee-high with green soy beans, grown so that us unproductive urban and suburbanite drones can be fed.

ODIFEROUS EASTERN ONTARIO FLATLANDS

When I'd set off from home I'd quickly popped the fuel cap, looked inside and seen gas slopping around, so I didn't give it much thought when I started out. Just after Chesterville the bike started to cough and splutter and soon stopped running at all. I wasn't too worried. I had a two-point-five litre plastic bottle in my pannier, so I was soon cruising again, assuming I might find fuel in Moose Creek, the next closest village. Moose Creek came and went without any signs of fuel. I was starting to get a little anxious. Crossing over Highway 417, I noticed a police cruiser idling at the side of the road. As I stopped opposite, he rolled down his window and I asked where the closest fuel might be found.

"You're closest is in Casselman," he replied, indicating that I would have to backtrack for five miles along the highway. That short trip was a little nerve racking. At any moment I expected to be stranded along the busy road, but I figured if the worst came to the worst, the friendly cop would be along eventually.

The Ottawa River at Hawkesbury was full to the brim. Over the previous few days the news had been full of reports about flooding along the Ottawa and St. Lawrence Rivers with people sand-bagging their houses and cottages in an optimistic attempt to protect their properties. Even the military had been drafted in to help.   As I rode east, circumventing Montreal, I crossed numerous small creeks and rivers, most of which had over run their banks and flooded the adjacent farm fields, creating a magical and unexpected playground for countless thousands of migrating geese.

It was a dull day. The sky and the water in the fields showing the same featureless grey. Even though it wasn't cold, the air temperature was cool enough that it began to seep through my multiple layers of riding gear and chill me. As I headed north up the Saint-Maurice River valley, I was happy to stop from time to time to take a few pictures and warm my chilled hands. Even though it was always unpleasant to pull off my outer gloves and the silk liners and expose my hands to the air while I fiddled with the cameras, it gave me an opportunity to stretch and bring some circulation back into my feet.

This wasn't going to be a mega-trip. I was expecting to be away from home no more that three or four days, as I had a very specific objective in mind.

Quebec Highway 155 follows the Saint-Maurice River for the whole distance between Shawinigan and La Tuque. The river is almost always visible, sometimes close, sometimes a short distance away, with rocky forested hills lining the valley. On a weekday in spring it's not too busy, but if the defacement of roadside cliffs with idiot names and mindless graffiti is anything to go by, it must be clogged with scenery-seekers later in the year, all eager to leave their 'I was here' mark on the landscape. I recommend birching or the stocks for the culprits – probably both.

Since the kind of people who think that defacing roadside rocks is appropriate never venture more than a few yards from their vehicles, most of the landscape is unblemished and attractive and the actions of a few mindless cretins does little to sour my mood or diminish the pleasure of the ride.

ALONG THE ST. MAURICE RIVER

As evening approached, I pulled into a motel at the edge of town, handed over my plastic and settled into the kind of small room budget conscious travellers and workers always head for. It wasn't exactly cheap – although the lady at reception had given me her best rate – and it had the essentials: a TV, a bed, hot water, shower and a toilet. A bottle of wine, some bread and local cheese from the nearby grocery store and the day was complete.

My GPS provided me with a convoluted route out of La Tuque, zig-zagging through suburban streets until I finally emerged back on to Highway 155 and was able to head north at a decent speed. Once again, the road was beside a river – this time the smaller Bostonnais River – a fast flowing, tea-coloured stream about thirty yards wide. At the small village of La Bostonnais I turned off the highway for a few yards just to ride across the covered bridge, before retracing my steps and continuing north. Traffic was light – just the occasional logging truck or pick-up – so stopping to take a few pictures along the route was stress-less and easy. Eventually, the river and the road diverged as Highway 155 continued north while the river's upper reaches lay further to the east within ZEC Kiskissink.

COVERED BRIDGE
AT LA BOSTONNAIS

As I continued north it started to become clear that spring had not really laid its grip on the landscape. Most of the lakes were still ice-bound, and the forest floor was covered in snow. Where the road swung close to one of the lakes, I parked the bike and walked down a steep slope to the lake shore, trudging through foot-deep icy snow to its frozen edge. Grey sky, grey ice and mist. It might have seemed a melancholy place had I not been so happy to be out in the world on my bike. I didn't fancy stepping on the ice though. It was probably fine, but it was starting to look punky and treacherous.

FROZEN LAKE - PUNK-IC

The miles drifted by. The Convert is a remarkably pleasant companion on such jaunts. For a start, it's dead comfortable. The big bars fall easily to hand, my knees form an almost perfect right-angle with my feet flat on the floorboards, and the seat is broad and plush. As I have long legs, I have raised the seat a little, using a sheepskin over a beaded seat cover to give me an extra half an inch of leg room, and added a foam wedge at the rear to pitch me slightly forwards. The end result is an all-day riding position that doesn't place too much pressure on the points of my buttocks – a common problem with many cruiser-style motorcycles.

When accelerating, the bike tends to sound odd. The revs rise quickly and stay there while the torque converter starts to catch up. By the time you've hit 55mph, which happens surprisingly quickly, the revs have mellowed and the engine note has died back to more normal decibels and you feel as though you're cruising in top gear. On long trips like this I'm rarely in a hurry, so 55mph is my favourite speed. It's fast enough to cover distance and not be an impediment to other road users, yet slow enough that you don't feel as though you are blistering through the landscape without taking any of it in.

Eventually, I crested the last rise and there in the distance was the full expanse of Lac St. Jean, its grey sheet of rotting ice looking menacing beneath the heavy clouds. It is an impressively-large body of water, some 25 miles long and 15 wide, which, along with the broad valley it occupies, exerts a moderating influence on the local weather. Not that you'd notice that much – it was still darn chilly in May, with a strong breeze driving ice-chilled air onshore. According to our friends at Wikipedia, the lake occupies the impact crater left by an asteroid, but you'll have to take their word for it because it wasn't obvious to me.

I had other things on my mind. My fingers were frozen and I needed fuel, both for the bike and for me. Foolishly I'd left La Tuque without any breakfast and my stomach was starting to complain about it.

The road that skirts around the south side of Lac St. Jean links a string of small towns. After about twenty minutes of cold, wet riding, I pulled in to the Tim Hortons parking lot at Métabetchouan-Lac-à-la-Croix, shut off the bike, waddled into the coffee shop and shed some of the multitudinous layers I was wearing before attempting to order or pee. Actually, the latter was rather more pressing than the former, but soon both had been attended to. I'm usually an eat-and-go kind of guy, but I must admit, I lingered rather longer over my coffee and sandwich than usual, as the heat started to work its way back into my extremities. I was fairly sure that the next leg of the ride – a short, high speed stint on the four-lane Highway 70 to Saguenay, followed by Highway 381 over the mountains – promised more cold and wet. I wasn't disappointed.

I'm not overly fond of major highways and avoid them whenever I can, but I do concede that they have their uses. If the purpose of Highway 70 is to whisk traffic through and past the suburbs of Jonquiere, Chicoutimi and Saguenay, then it does an admirable job. I dropped briefly down to the small town of La Baie just to get a glimpse of the Saguenay Fjord but didn't linger long. Perhaps I should have. I subsequently found out that much of the downtown was seriously damaged during July 1996 when heavy rain upstream filled the rivers eventually leading to the failure of the dam on Ha! Ha! Lake. The subsequent torrents of water washed away houses and bridges and destroyed much of the downtown.

But I was eager to ride on. The northern part of Highway 381 lies within the Saguenay-Lac Saint-Jean tourist region while the southern half is within the Charlevoix region. This didn't mean much to me. Having looked at sections of the road on Google Streetview, I knew I could expect plenty of trees, plenty of sweeping curves, and a few rounded hills gradually morphing into low mountains the closer I got to the Parc national des Grands-Jardins about 60 miles further south.

For the first little while the roadside was sprinkled with small bungalows and houses – the kind that lie along most roads which pass through areas close enough to a city to be within commuter distance. Soon enough though, I'd left the populated areas behind as the road headed into the hills. On a really fast bike, with dry roads and an almost zero likelihood of encountering any police, 381 must be a real blast. I, however, wasn't riding a really fast bike, the roads were sodden, my rear tire was almost bald and I have little interest in high speed riding at the best of times. I plodded along catching sight of the occasional frozen lake through the trees, enjoying the sound of the Guzzi's pipes reverberating off the occasional rock-cut, the spatter of rain drops on my windshield and visor and the hiss of the tires on the road. Each time the road climbed a hill I would enter a misty cloud-world of water droplets and rain, where snow lay deep in the bush and along the margins of the highway. My main preoccupation became keeping my visor clear. Each time the road dropped to lower elevations the precipitation and road-side snow would vanish and I would catch a glimpse of mist-shrouded mountain tops to either side.

Eastern Canada doesn't have the precipitous and visually stunning mountain ranges found on the west side of the continent. Those are upstart mountains. On the scale of geological time they are newcomers, created less than 100 million years ago. The mountains on the east side of the continent are much, much older and have been worn down to mere stumps and fragments of their former selves. 500 million years and countless periods of glaciation and erosion have rounded, smoothed and softened the appearance of the Laurentians (of which those I was passing through are a part). Make no mistake, there are still some substantial lumps but they lack the jagged-tooth appearance of their western counterparts.

ANCIENT STUMPS OF MOUNTAINS

I find the upland landscape of Quebec, the Maritimes and the adjacent states of Maine and Vermont to be charming, if not desperately dramatic. While most are tree clad and smooth-sided, there are just enough precipitous slopes and rugged fractured rock exposures to keep the eye interested.

Then there's the smell. There is a distinctive late-winter/early spring odour to those upland forests: a combination of bruised cedar and spruce mixed with the moisture-laden air which drifts across melting lake ice and decaying snow. I love it. It alone was worth riding 500 miles for.

I pulled into a roadside viewing area and climbed the steps up to the overlook. There were few sounds in the still air: the caw of a crow in the distance, the rustle of a junco in a nearby bush; otherwise all was serene. Across the frozen lake the closest mountain was cloaked in spruce on one side and the soft, light-grey haze of leafless maple, poplar and birch on the other. I wondered whether this was because of differences in climate and soils, or whether the steeper areas where the spruce were growing had just been too uneconomical to harvest.

I had been rolling again for a few minutes when I caught sight of a stocky dark shape in my peripheral vision. I immediately braked hard, did a quick u-turn and was just in time to see the blackest porcupine I have ever seen waddle anxiously across a bush track and into the safety of the forest. I like porcupines; they are slow, a bit dopey and totally harmless as long as you're not stupid enough to get within range of their tail. Sadly, their self-protection strategy of turning their well-armed rear towards danger doesn't work well against motor vehicles. They are frequent casualties on the roads. This fellow was heading away from the road, so I left him to his own adventures and carried on with mine.

As I passed over the highest elevations where the surrounding uplands of the Pied-des-Monts reach heights of over 1000 metres and even the road crawls up to 896 metres, the mists quickly turned to rain. I was still stopping from time to time to manage my video cameras and take stills, so I took the opportunity to pull my rain gear on. This was the terrain I'd come to see, and I wasn't disappointed. The road was suitably quiet, curvaceous and well paved, the mountains felt ancient and wild, and if the weather was a bit grim, it only added to the whole atmosphere.

Each time I stopped, the Convert was reluctant to start again unless I gave it a big handful of throttle, and it wouldn't idle reliably. A quick road-side adjustment of the points-gap soon had the bike behaving properly, and I was able to ride on through the rain towards Baie Sainte-Paul and the St. Lawrence River coastline.

By the time I reached Baie Sainte-Paul the rain had changed from a light spattering – more of a heavy mist really – to a full-blown, heavy downpour. My multi-layer cold, rain and wind protection was holding well, although I could feel the chill of dampness creeping up my sleeves and down the front of my neck. There was little point in stopping. The rain was quite obviously in for the rest of the day, so I carried on, following Highway 138 – the old road that hugs the north shore of the St. Lawrence – most of the way to Quebec City.

Old Quebec City is a wonderful place. The walled city has a European feel with a French-Canadian twist which makes it unique, but it was no place for me on a wet spring afternoon. I avoided the road signs which lead you downtown; instead, I allowed myself to be guided towards the multi-lane Highway 40 which loops through the industrial sprawl to the north. I was hoping to sail through easily, but traffic was extremely heavy and areas of roadwork slowed the vehicles in many places.

Despite the heavy rain and the spray from endless large trucks, the Convert resolutely plugged along without showing any signs of distress. And, once again, I was happy to see that Quebec drivers are generally respectful of motorbikes, giving me plenty of space and consideration.

During the earlier part of this ride I hadn't given much thought to which bike I was riding, but, as the density of traffic increased around Quebec City, I realized I was awfully happy I had decided to ride the Convert. All along the Saint-Maurice Valley and up Highway 155 to Saguenay, then back down 381 to Baie Saint-Paul, it really wouldn't have mattered which bike I was riding. Gear changes are few and far between. It's all easy top-gear riding for mile after mile. In those situations, the Convert is almost indistinguishable from its geared relatives. Where the Convert really shines is in heavy stop-and-go traffic or in conditions where a jerky gear change could easily result in a loss of traction. With sheets of water washing across the road, this was a real possibility.

At each obstruction through Quebec, I would simply roll off the throttle and gently apply the foot brake. The linked brakes provided smooth, secure deceleration with enough power to really pull the bike up quickly if a sudden change in traffic tempo caught me unawares. With no gears to fuss with the Convert is always in the right gear, accelerating smoothly and without any jerkiness from any speed. In difficult conditions, not having to fuss with gears and clutch made for easy riding through heavy traffic in some of the wettest rain I've ever encountered, and helped me stay calm and safe. I know you're probably thinking 'I have no problems with gears in wet weather,' and neither do I, but, until you've ridden without them, you don't know how easy life can be.

Ironically, I have nothing but contempt for cars with automatic transmissions and recently bought a VW Golf Wagon with a six-speed manual gearbox just because it's more fun to drive than any slush-box counterpart. On a bike though, it's a different thing. Try it, you might be surprised.

Once through the worst of the traffic hold-ups, I rejoined Highway 138 and enjoyed a less stressful ride. An hour outside Quebec City I'd had enough. My leather gloves, which have no water-resistance at all, were soaked through and my hands were freezing. Water had found its way into my usually-waterproof, gore-tex lined ex-army boots, my knees were cold and my chest was soaked. I pulled in to the first motel I saw, on the outskirts of Portneuf. I was done for the day.

A BRIEF RESPITE FROM THE RAIN

It was still raining the next morning. My clothes hadn't dried much over night so it was a somewhat soggy Nick that hit the road again. Despite sitting naked and alone in an unremitting downpour, the Convert started instantly and we were soon gliding serenely down the road. The return ride was almost a replay of the first day; I skirted Montreal, crossed the Ottawa River at Hawkesbury, then took back-roads across eastern Ontario to home.

Somewhere along the route I noticed that my indicators weren't flashing when I signaled. The lights would light up if I manually switched the switch, so it was obvious that the flasher unit itself had failed. Darn unreliable Guzzis.

I had only just noticed this when I passed a Yamaha dealer selling motorbikes, ATVs and snowmachines so I pulled the offending flasher unit from behind the side panel and walked in.

"Do you have one of these?" I said, showing him the flasher unit – the kind that virtually every vehicle on the planet has tucked away under the dash.

"What's it from? Do you have a part number? We do everything by part numbers".

I may have sounded a bit exasperated as I said,

"It's an automotive flasher unit. They're on just about every vehicle ever made. This one is off my old Guzzi".

"No, sorry. Unless you've got a part number........"

I couldn't believe it. I rode on, stopped at the next little town with a Canadian Tire, picked one off the shelf, plugged it in to the bike, checked that the indicators now worked (they did), and carried on towards home.

The rain had finally stopped and the remaining hours of this little three-day trip passed on dry uncrowded roads in pleasant sunshine. My rear bungee net swelled with rain gear I no longer needed, and the dampness which had made its way up the sleeves of my leather jacket and down the front gradually dried out. It was nice not to be fighting traffic, rain and water-sloshed roads. The rain of the previous couple of days had done little to diminish the pungency of the freshly manured fields to either side of the road, but I didn't mind. I was humming along in comfort, the Convert's lazy engine eating up the miles.

You can cover a lot of ground in three days. I'd explored a road that had been on my 'to do' list for quite a while and ridden over a thousand miles in comfort and style on a 43 year old classic without any significant problems or issues. The Convert may not be everyone's idea of an ideal touring ride, but it works for me.

And while some people may find riding old bikes to distant places an odd way to spend one's time, full of potential danger and discomfort, to me, sitting on the couch doing nothing is far more dangerous. Show me an old bike and an interesting road and I'm off, and to heck with the weather and the potential for roadside breakdowns.

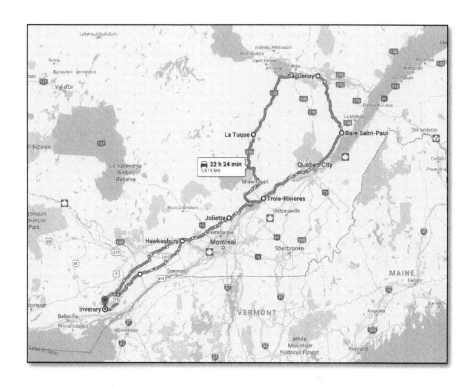

ABOUT THE AUTHOR

Nick Adams emigrated to Canada from the UK in 1977 to work for the Ontario government as an archaeologist. He soon fell in love with Canada's north and, for the past few years, has been exploring it by canoe and on his beloved 1970's Moto Guzzi motorcycles.

Over the years, as the number of bikes in his garage has increased, so have his travels in Canada as he seeks out distant places and deserted highways. Eschewing modern adventure bikes, Nick prefers to ride his older bikes, arguing that a few road-side breakdowns and 'tune-up's' are an integral part of any adventure.

From time to time, he returns to the UK to 'get a breath of Britain' by hiking some of its many long-distance footpaths and riding around visiting friends and relatives on rented motorbikes.   Writing about his trips and sharing them with others doubles the pleasure. He is a regular contributor to 'RealClassic' magazine and frequently posts to on-line motorcycle forums.

BOOKS BY THE SAME AUTHOR

<u>Beyond the Coffee Shop: Riding 1970's Moto Guzzi Motorcycles in Northern Canada</u>

"Canada is blessed with thousands of kilometres of empty roads which seem to wind on forever through forested hills and between still blue lakes. What better way to explore them than by riding 40 year old Italian motorbikes, famous for their dodgy electrics and sparse dealer network. 40 year old bikes, aged rider, thousands of kilometres of virtually unserviced empty roads in the middle of bear, wolf and blackfly infested wilderness - what could possibly go wrong?"

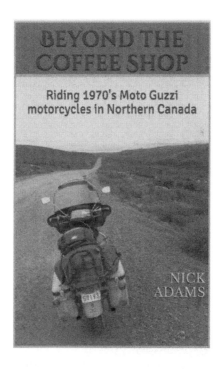

Beyond the Bypass: Life and Motorcycling after Heart Surgery

When you're standing on the edge of the abyss, health failing, the idea of being sliced open down the middle for heart surgery may not seem terribly appealing, but most people agree, it's probably preferable to the alternative. Despite a lifetime of healthy outdoor activity and a diet no worse (or better for that matter) than the next man's, in 2017, at the age of 66, Nick found himself under the knife for triple bypass surgery. Would this be the end to hiking adventures and long motorcycle trips to remote parts? Not a chance! Recovery from open heart surgery is a long, slow process, but with plenty of help, some dedication, lots of careful walking, and heaps of good luck, it is possible to return to a fully active life. This book describes Nick's experiences with 'CABG' (Coronary Artery Bypass Graft) and his eventual return to doing those things he loves. If you are having, or have just had CABG, hold on to the belief that there is light at the end of the tunnel. And when you are able to return to the activities you enjoy, they will seem more worthwhile and precious than before.

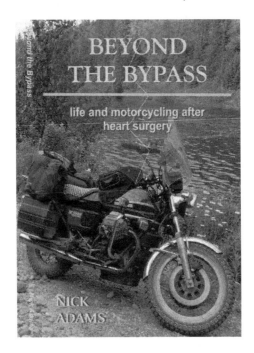

The Road to Missinabie: and other motorcycle road tales

The Road to Missanabie is Nick Adams's second collection of motorcycling road tales. Join Nick as he heads for the horizon in northern Quebec and northern Ontario on his old Moto Guzzi bikes, enjoying the vastness of the northern forests, the quiet of northern lakes and the generous and friendly company of the people he meets.

Things don't always go according to plan, but unexpected hiccups and delays along the way just add to the adventure.

THE ROAD TO
MISSANABIE

and other motorcycle road tales

NICK
ADAMS

<u>Actually, I'm English: rediscovering my homeland on foot and by motorcycle</u>

"Forty years is a long time to be away. Travelling on foot and by motorbike, Nick Adams discovers that while many things have changed, the things he loved; the hills, the pubs, the back roads and yes, even the weather, are undiminished. Join Nick as he hikes the length of Wales, hitting all the high spots. Then follow him up the spine of England on the Pennine Way, through brutal February weather. On his third trip, circumstances conspire against him. The original plan was to walk from Chepstow all the way to the Lake District. It didn't quite work out that way. Lastly, follow Nick across the North York Moors at night, then on across the country to the Cumbria coast. As if the snow, rain and endless miles weren't enough while hiking, jump on the back of the motorbike and ride from Scotland to Devon via Norfolk, dodging hypothermia, then through the Lakes, the Pennines and Wales. Nick's idea of a good time seems to involve bad weather, difficult terrain, stealth camping and innumerable pubs. This is one man's view of a country he loves, told in a simple, engaging style. Come along for the ride."

ARCHAEOLOGY - Life in the Trenches: It Ain't All Golden Masks and Crystal Skulls

Archaeology is a beguiling occupation. Who wouldn't be attracted to finding cool, old stuff buried in the ground? It appeals to the child in us all. But archaeology isn't all gold masks, crystal skulls and temples. Often it's chert flakes on a lake shore, burials in the forgotten corner of a field, or pioneer dwellings in the woods. Sometimes it just isn't all that glamorous. The reality is that for every well-known archaeologist - the kind you might see doing exciting things on TV - there are legions of less high-profile characters working in the background. Their work may not be quite as sexy or result in paradigm-changing discoveries, but it is important and valuable. The following chapters are snap-shots of archaeology from more than forty years of work in both Britain and Canada. Rather than spending too much time on the scientific and technical, Nick has focussed on stories which convey the life of a working archaeologist ...... well, his working life anyway.

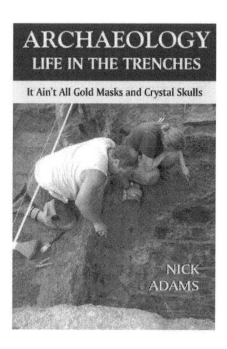